The SINGLE MOM Journey

A 30 Day Devotional Guide

Sean P. Teis

Connie M. Teis

LIFE FACTORS MINISTRIES
preventing & helping broken homes

LIFE FACTORS MINISTRIES
preventing & helping broken homes

The Single Mom Journey

A Personal Devotional and Church Small Group Resource

By

Sean P. Teis

with

Connie M. Teis

©2012 Life Factors Ministries

Printed in the United States of America   ISBN: 978-1-937129-60-6

The quoted ideas expressed in this book (but not Scripture verses) are not, in all cases, exact quotations, as some have been edited for clarity and brevity. In all cases, the author has attempted to maintain the speaker's original intent. In some cases, quoted material for this book was obtained from secondary sources, primarily print media. While every effort was made to ensure the accuracy of these sources, the accuracy cannot be guaranteed. For additions, deletions, corrections, or clarifications in the future editions of this text, please write Life Factors Ministries.

Scripture quotations are taken from: King James Version

THE SINGLE MOM JOURNEY

THE SINGLE MOM JOURNEY

TO:

_____

FROM:

_____

DATE:

_____

DEDICATION

This book is dedicated to three of the most wonderful children in the world. They are the reason I persevered and made it through my Single Mom Journey. I would also like to dedicate this book to my son-in-law, daughter-in-laws, and my beautiful grandchildren. Lastly, to my many friends, family, and church family who helped me on my journey, but most of all to my Heavenly Father for blessing me with my three children and for giving me daily strength to make it through. Romans 8:28 "And we know that all things work together for good to them that love God, to them who are the called according to his purpose."

- Connie

It was truly a blessing to write this book with my mother; it gave me additional insight into the sacrifices that she made for which I am truly grateful. I dedicate this book to my wife and two precious sons who are my greatest earthly assets! I would like to especially thank Emily and Jackie for helping us shape this book into perfection. May God use this resource to provide eternal hope to single moms all over the world! I Thessalonians 5:24 "Faithful is he that calleth you, who also will do it."

- Sean

CHURCHES

For assistance in launching and maintaining a single mom small group at your church please visit lifefactors.org! We look forward to partnering with you in ministering to the single moms in your local church and community! Check out our site today!

TRIP SCHEDULE

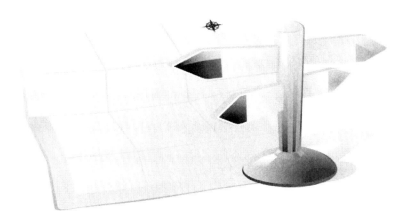

Preparation

Day 1 – Let's Talk About God

Day 2 – So, You Are A Single Mom

Day 3 – Depression

Day 4 – You Are Not Alone

Day 5 – You Are Loved

Day 6 – Talking To God

Day 7 – Overcoming Fear

Day 8 – Dealing With Discouragement

Day 9 – Trusting God

The Trip – Week 1 – The Beginning (Internal Change)

Day 10 – Forgiveness

Day 11 – Inferiority

Day 12 – Outcast

Day 13 – Envy

Day 14 – Giving It All To God

Day 15 – Mistakes

Day 16 – Purity Of Mind And Heart

The Trip – Week 2 – The Middle (External Change)
Day 17 – Purity Of Body
Day 18 – Unselfish
Day 19 – Thankfulness
Day 20 – Finding Security
Day 21 – Overcoming Abuse
Day 22 – Breaking The Cycle
Day 23 – God Brings Happiness

The Trip – Week 3 – The End (Your Future)
Day 24 – Confidence
Day 25 – Father's Day
Day 26 – Mentors – For You
Day 27 – Mentors – For Your Children
Day 28 – Church
Day 29 – Setting Goals
Day 30 – Success

WELCOME

Hello!

Welcome to the Single Mom Journey! Somehow you ended up on this journey and we are here to help you continue on! When you became a single mom the feelings were probably as if someone gave you a suitcase that weighed a thousand pounds and told you to start walking. Included in this journey there were no instructions, no time estimation, and quite frankly not much help at all. So, now you are here, perhaps feeling all alone looking at this journey and thinking to yourself, how will I complete this thing?

Well, there is good news; this book is designed to help you along your individual journey. There are certain issues you are facing or will be facing as a single mom and they need to be addressed. You need preparation, because the trip isn't going to be easy, and it isn't always fun, but with a little help and guidance you can make it through! I have taken the knowledge of my mother's personal experience and have polled others, so that on the next 30 days we can focus on the key elements that will most likely hinder you on your journey.

CHOICES – CHOICES – CHOICES

So now you have the following two choices:

1. You can lie down and be defeated and never conquer this journey, dealing with the consequences for the rest of your life.

-OR-

2. You can get started, conquer this life circumstance, and put this journey behind you as much as possible.

That is right; it is your decision. You alone decide what path you will take for the rest of your life, and you must get through this journey in order to move on. You can't ignore it, because it is staring you right in the face. To live a successful life you must confront this situation, and begin dealing with it, and I hope that you will. I am positive that you will make the right decision, and I cannot wait until I see you on the other side of this mountain. Have a great trip!

You know, you have the ability to conquer this journey and continue on successfully with the rest of your life. What are you waiting for? Go ahead and begin with day 1. I will be praying for you! You will not regret taking this journey with us!

Your Friend,

Sean Teis
President
Life Factors Ministries

P.S. If you have any questions or need help along your journey please contact us through email at info@lifefactors.org or on Facebook at facebook.com/lifefactorsministries, and we will try our best to help!

The Single Mom Journey

lifefactors.org

Visit our website to find additional helpful resources! We are here for you and want to help you along your single mom journey! Check out the site today!

PREPARATION

Days 1-9

The Single Mom Journey
Day 1

Let's Talk About God

"For God so loved the world, that he gave his only begotten Son, that whosoever believeth in him should not perish, but have everlasting life." John 3:16

When I was growing up my parents always made us go to Sunday School and church, it did not matter if we were up late the night before they still made us go. Going to church instilled in me a belief of God, but it was not until I was an adult that I truly understood what Christianity was all about. I got married in 1975 when I was 24 years old. Shortly after, my husband and I moved from my home town in Central Pennsylvania to his hometown of Las Vegas, Nevada. This move made me nervous, home sick, and worried. I was truly a small town girl moving to a big city. Little did I know, this move would force me to make the biggest decision of my life. Soon after moving to Las Vegas, my mother-in-law, a devout Christian, insisted that I go to church with her. Eventually, I agreed to go to a revival service. I will never forget the song we sang that night titled, "Heaven Came Down and Glory Filled My Soul," and I was blessed to find out what this really meant. At this service, I realized that I was a lost sinner on my way to an eternity in Hell, and that by accepting a personal relationship with Jesus Christ I could know for sure that I would go to Heaven someday when I died. After the preacher was finished with his sermon I went forward and made the most important decision that I have ever made. I asked Jesus to come into my heart to save me! I also realized that just going to church, as I did as a child, was not enough; we need to have a personal relationship with Jesus Christ. How wonderful it is to know for sure that I will go to Heaven when I die. You too have the ability to decide where you will go when you die. If you have never accepted Christ as your personal Savior, follow the steps on the next page in the challenge section. Your decision of where you will spend eternity is the most important decision that you will ever make.

–Connie

Challenge ~ Day 1

Where you will go when you die is the most important decision you will ever make. That is right; it is your decision. You also get to decide whether or not you want a relationship with your Heavenly Father. Being a single mom is a hard journey, but through a relationship with your Heavenly Father there is hope. The first step on the Single Mom Journey is confirming that you have a relationship with the Lord Jesus Christ. God wants you to rest in Him as your Heavenly Father. He will never leave or forsake you (Hebrews 13:5). All you must do is accept His Son, the Lord Jesus Christ as your personal Savior. John 3:16 shows us that God loved us so much that He made a way for us to go to Heaven by sending His only begotten Son. The following verses will show you how to accept this free gift that He is offering to you:

> **1. Romans 3:23** *"for all have sinned, and come short of the glory of God."* – You must realize that you are a sinner. Have you ever lied, cheated, used a curse word, or hated someone? If so, then you have sinned, and admitting you are a sinner is the first step. Every person has sinned.
> **2. Romans 6:23a** *"For the wages of sin is death;"* – The punishment for your sin is eternal death in Hell.
> **3. Romans 5:8** *"But God commendeth his love toward us, in that, while we were yet sinners, Christ died for us."* – Out of God's love for us, He sent His Son to die for our sins. This is our hope, through Christ we can be saved from an eternal death.
> **4. Romans 6:23b** *"but the gift of God is eternal life through Jesus Christ our Lord."* – God's gift is eternal life in Heaven through Jesus Christ.
> **5. Romans 10:13** *"For whosoever shall call upon the name of the Lord shall be saved."* – You must accept the gift by faith believing in Jesus and asking Him to come into your heart. If you understand this information and would like to ask Jesus into your heart, please pray the suggested prayer in the Prayer Time section.

 # Going Further

In one or two sentences describe what John 3:16 means to you?

How has John 3:16 helped you on your single mom journey?

What is your salvation testimony? If you just trusted in Christ then write about that!

Have your children trusted Christ as their personal Savior? If they have, how do you plan to help them grow in their faith? If they have not, how do you plan on teaching them about Jesus? Write a plan of action.

 # Take Action

In your first prayer journal entry, write out a thank you letter to God for sending His Son to die for your sins.

Prayer Time

Prayer Requests:

_____

_____

_____

_____

_____

_____

Suggested Prayer:

Dear Lord Jesus, I know that I am a sinner. I know that You are God, and I know that You died in my place to pay for my sin. I believe that You rose from the dead, proving that You are God. Right now, in the best way that I know how, I call upon You and ask You to be my Lord and my Savior and my God. Thank You Jesus for dying for me. Help me now to live for You...

The Single Mom Journey

The Single Mom Journey

Day 2

So, You Are A Single Mom

"Not that I speak in respect of want: for I have learned, in whatsoever state I am, therewith to be content." Philippians 4:11

It was a summer night in 1985, we were living back in my hometown in Central Pennsylvania, and my husband came home in a drunken rage. He woke up our three children, and slapped our daughter across the face for crying because he woke her up. Then he threw my oldest son Jerry, my daughter April, and I out of our home, but for some reason he kept our nine month old son Sean with him. In a panic, we ran over to the neighbors and called my sister who called the police for us. The police arrived and they were able to get into our home. The police then asked my husband to hand my youngest son over to them, and he obliged, but instead of gently handing him over he threw him across the room to the police. Thankfully that officer could catch! The police told him that if they ever had to come back again they would take him to jail. A few days later, my husband decided to take a one way bus trip back to Las Vegas, never to return again. So there I was now a single mom with three young children to take care of, and there was no manual to follow. When the bus drove away I instantly was filled with shock, fear, rejection, sadness, and many feelings that took me several years to overcome, but then we walked to the car and drove home. From this day forward I did my best, please understand that I was not in any way perfect as a single mom, but through God's grace we made it through. Regardless of where you are in your single mom journey it is crucial to find your contentment in God and God alone. I challenge you to stick to it, do not give up, because in the end you will not regret it!

-Connie

Challenge ~ Day 2

Let's face it, just being a single mom is sometimes quite overwhelming. Along with the many life-altering results of a single parent home it may at times make you feel hopeless. You may be asking yourself several questions such as: How will I raise my children on my own? How will I afford to do this alone? Who will I talk to when I feel alone? Remember that God is always here for you! The reality is that you may not have anyone in your life to help you on this journey, but you have been given a unique life path. You must remember that even though you are now a single mom and have been given a hard job it is also a very rewarding job. Your children need you, and right now raising them is God's will for your life. Once you realize that you are a single mom, and that God wants you to complete this task, it is then time to get going and not give up! This obligation has been given to you and you are the best person for the job! Being a single mom is not always a fun situation, and at times can be hard to face, but remember you can get through it. As you prepare for this journey, start thinking about contentment. What are the things in your life that you could be thankful for? What things has God saved you from? You must accept the situation that God has given you and learn to be content. Follow today's theme verse and begin to practice contentment in all situations you are given: Philippians 4:11 *"Not that I speak in respect of want: for I have learned, in whatsoever state I am, therewith to be content."* Get going!

 # Going Further

In one or two sentences describe what Philippians 4:11 means to you?

How has Philippians 4:11 helped you on your single mom journey?

What are three things you and your children have had to learn to overcome or accept during this journey?

Write out your story, how did you get to where you are now? Part of your healing is in talking about and working through your circumstances.

 # Take Action

Write out the things that you have to be content or thankful about in your life. Remember that there are others who have a harder situation to work through.

☎ Prayer Time

Prayer Requests:

_____

_____

_____

_____

_____

_____

_____

Suggested Prayer:

Dear God, help me to be content in the single mom journey I am on. Help me to be thankful for the things that You have given to me and not to worry about the things I may be missing. I thank You today for the blessings that You have given me, and I pray that You would give me strength for the shortcomings...

The Single Mom Journey

The Single Mom Journey
Day 3

<u>Depression</u>

"And he said unto me, My grace is sufficient for thee: for my strength is made perfect in weakness. Most gladly therefore will I rather glory in my infirmities, that the power of Christ may rest upon me." II Corinthians 12:9

When I was growing up divorce was almost unheard of. Most homes consisted of a husband and a wife doing their part in the home. This was definitely not the case in our home; I was doing it all, and often times it got overwhelming. Frankly, it was depressing. Depression is one of the biggest struggles for single moms, because we do not have that person to partner with along the parenting journey. I was dealing with the rejection of losing a husband that I sincerely loved, I was trying to hide my feelings and be strong for my children, and I was lonely. I was in a continual state of being overwhelmed. When I got depressed it was very hard for me to function; I did what I had to, but beyond that I struggled. I constantly questioned why it happened to me. About a month after he left, we had to move out of our home and into my parents' house due to finances. In addition, I had to begin working more hours and figure out what I was going to do with my children while I was not there. I know what it feels like to seemingly be in the depths of despair without seeing an exit, but there is hope. To overcome depression I continued to take my children to church and most importantly have a relationship with God. A week after my husband left, I was attending a ladies Bible study and it was there that my cousin announced my situation and the group began to pray for me. After this event, my Pastor's mother gave me some money and said that God told her to give it to me. Shortly thereafter, I counseled with my Pastor and he taught me that through God's Grace I would conquer this situation and he quoted II Corinthians 12:9. From that day forward every time he saw me he said "God's Grace" or "Remember God's Grace," I believed this then and I believe it now. This verse applies to you as well, through God's Grace you can conquer the continual battle with depression that a single mom may face.

-Connie

Challenge ~ Day 3

Depression: what thoughts came into your mind when you read that word? Perhaps you thought: "that's my life," "I know someone like that," or "I feel that way at times." Depression is not easy and can be brought on through a wide variety of reasons. "In the U.S. about 15 million people experience depression each year. The majority of them are women. Unfortunately, nearly two-thirds do not get the help they need."[1] So what exactly does the world say about depression? The following is a definition from the Mayo Clinic: *"More than just a bout of the blues, depression isn't a weakness, nor is it something that you can simply "snap out" of. Depression is a chronic illness that usually requires long-term treatment, like diabetes or high blood pressure. But don't get discouraged. Most people with depression feel better with medication, psychological counseling or other treatment."*[2] Wow, after reading this definition depression is a serious situation. Please understand by reading this book it will not provide medication or even psychological counseling for that matter, but this book is about the "other treatment" that was mentioned in this definition. Sometimes individuals may be at the point where they need medicine or psychological counseling (if this is your current situation we advise you to seek the medical help you need), but in some situations it is the "other treatment" that the individual facing depression needs. The Bible says *"My grace is sufficient for thee: for my strength is made perfect in weakness. Most gladly therefore will I rather glory in my infirmities, that the power of Christ may rest upon me."* When you are facing depression, as many individuals do, God will be there to help you through it. The next time you are feeling depressed, seek the grace of God, because His grace will guide, strengthen, encourage, direct, comfort, and provide fulfillment in your life!

 # Going Further

In one or two sentences describe what II Corinthians 12:9 means to you?

How has II Corinthians 12:9 helped you on your single mom journey?

What is an inspiring song, Bible verse, poem, or something similar that uplifts and encourages you when depression strikes?

In your own words define depression?

Write a paragraph about someone (friend, family member, celebrity, Bible character, etc.) who could not overcome depression. Why did they struggle with depression? Why weren't they able to overcome it? What could they have done differently?

Write a paragraph about someone (friend, family member, celebrity, Bible character, etc.) who struggled with depression and overcame it. Why did they struggle with depression? How did they overcome it? How can you learn from their situation?

Take Action

Write an encouraging letter to yourself. That is right, write a letter to yourself filled with encouragement for the next time you are feeling depressed. In this letter include Scripture, testimonies of when God's grace appeared, encouraging songs, etc. Then when you are feeling depression arise in your life, pull out this letter and read it out loud reminding yourself of God's blessings, comfort, strength, and other important attributes of His blessed grace.

Prayer Time

Prayer Requests:

_____

_____

_____

_____

_____

_____

Suggested Prayer:

Dear Lord, thank You for giving me hope in You. Despite the circumstance I may face on this earth, I will be glorified together with You someday. I thank You for giving me the understanding that all things will work together through You. Please give me strength to continually put You first...

The Single Mom Journey

The Single Mom Journey
Day 4

You Are Not Alone

"Let your conversation be without covetousness; and be content with such things as ye have: for he hath said, I will never leave thee, nor forsake thee." Hebrews 13:5

I can honestly say I know what it is like to be lonely. I know what it is like to be in a room full of people and still feel alone. No longer having a husband, I even hated going shopping or anywhere that involved me being alone and surrounded by couples. It always seemed as though I was the only one alone. It was a trick Satan played on my mind that took a long time to overcome. I did my best to concentrate on my children and have fun with them. I had to realize that they were hurting too. I have to say that God truly blessed me with a large extended family, a church family, and many friends. A lot of people were there for us on the journey. I am so thankful for listening ears and caring people especially on those days that I felt overwhelmingly alone. I had a hard time feeling I had to have a man in my life. God showed me that I needed to replace the loneliness of being single with other activities such as spending time with family and old friends, watching old TV shows, reading books, doing word searches, writing out greeting cards to others, etc. More importantly God showed me that I needed to focus on Him and not think about not having a husband. I had to learn that my happiness did not come from a person but from God. There were times when I felt God didn't care, but as His Word says, *"I will never leave thee nor forsake thee."* The best person you can talk to is God. He always cares, He always has time for you, and He will always listen to what you have to say.

-Connie

Challenge ~ Day 4

Do you ever feel like you are all alone on your own personal island, as if no one understands you and your situation, or as if you are the only person on planet earth going through this single mom experience? When the word island is mentioned today many individuals think of the old television show, Gilligan's Island. If you have never heard of this show, it was about a group of individuals that were stranded on a deserted island, displaying in a comical format how they survived and their attempts to get off of the island. The following is part of their theme song:

> Just sit right back and you'll hear a tale, a tale of a fateful trip
> That started from this tropic port, aboard this tiny Ship.
> The mate was a mighty sailin' man, the Skipper brave and sure,
> Five passengers set sail that day for a three hour tour.
> A three hour tour.
> The weather started getting rough, the tiny ship was tossed.
> If not for the courage of the fearless crew, the Minnow would be lost.
> The Minnow would be lost...[3]

Though you may feel like Gilligan, all alone on your individual island, you must realize you are never alone. Hebrews 13:5 assures us of this in saying, *"for he hath said, I will never leave thee, nor forsake thee."* When you feel most alone remember God is always there waiting for you!

 # Going Further

In one or two sentences describe what Hebrews 13:5 means to you?

How has Hebrews 13:5 helped you on your single mom journey?

What are some activities that you could partake in to replace the feeling of loneliness on your journey? Examples would be: spending time with family and old friends, reading books, prayer and Bible study, scrapbooking, etc.

Where does your happiness come from?

Is God the center of your happiness? If He is, describe in what ways. If He is not, what are ways you could make a change?

 # Take Action

Make a list of the times you feel most alone. Begin to ask God to give you strength and comfort to overcome those times.

☎ Prayer Time

Prayer Requests:

_____

_____

_____

_____

_____

_____

Suggested Prayer:

Dear Lord, please help me today to be aware of Your presence. Help me to remember that You are always there when I may feel alone, because Your Scriptures say You will never leave me nor forsake me...

The Single Mom Journey

The Single Mom Journey
Day 5

You Are Loved

"I am crucified with Christ: nevertheless I live; yet not I, but Christ liveth in me: and the life which I now live in the flesh I live by the faith of the Son of God, who loved me, and gave himself for me." Galatians 2:20

"To have and to hold from this day forward, for better or for worse, for richer, for poorer, in sickness and in health, to love and to cherish; from this day forward until death do us part." On my wedding day my husband said something similar to this, and it turned out to only be a lie. I was able to overcome most of it, but one of the hardest parts to overcome was that he did not stay committed to the "love and to cherish" part. Feeling unloved is common as a single mom, but always remember that your children love you, and most importantly that God loves you. One of my favorite hymns is "And Can It Be That I Should Gain." The following are some of the lyrics of this song:

> *"And can it be that I should gain*
> *An interest in the Savior's blood?*
> *Died He for me, who caused His pain—*
> *For me, who Him to death pursued?*
> *Amazing love! How can it be,*
> *That Thou, my God, shouldst die for me?"[A]*

This song shows us that God loves us no matter what, no matter what we do, no matter where we go, God loves us. Another aspect of love is that your children need to know that you love them. Do not ever let a lack of love you feel keep you from loving your children with your whole being! Embrace them, hug them, kiss them, tell them that you love them, and most importantly tell them God loves them. In doing this you will instill a sense of love in your home. Remember that the Bible says that God is love. I John 4:7 says *"Beloved, let us love one another: for love is of God; and every one that loveth is born of God, and knoweth God."* I challenge you today to be loving toward others and remember that God always loves you!

−Connie

Challenge ~ Day 5

Take a moment to think about what you believe love is. Many people differ on their opinion of love. For all of us love is a needed act or gift toward us. When we know we are loved our day is better and the sun seems to shine a little brighter. What happens though when we do not feel loved? As a single mom you probably desire love. You know that your children love you, but what about that companion that many other women have? For many women this is hard to deal with, but do not ever get yourself into a position where your pursuit of love from a man ruins the love you have for your children or the love that your children have for you. No matter how unloved you may feel at times, you should be comforted to know that Christ loves you. He loved you so much that He was severely beaten, crucified on a cross, stabbed in the side with a sword, spat upon, forced to wear a crown of thorns, mocked, and ultimately persecuted. He loves us so much that He died for us. Galatians 2:20 tells us that as Christians we are *"crucified with Christ."* Many times our lives will not be easy, but we can rest assured that no matter what problems we will face we have the ability to get through them simply by resting in the love of Christ.

 # Going Further

In one or two sentences describe what Galatians 2:20 means to you?

How has Galatians 2:20 helped you on your single mom journey?

What is another verse in the Bible that shows you that God loves you?

What is your definition of love?

What are some ways that you show your children that you love them? What are some additional ways that you could show love to them?

How can a single mother show God's love to her children?

 # Take Action

Write a letter to Jesus thanking Him for His love and how His love has helped you overcome downfalls in your life.

_____
_____
_____
_____
_____
_____
_____
_____
_____
_____
_____
_____
_____
_____
_____
_____
_____
_____
_____
_____
_____
_____

Prayer Time

Prayer Requests:

_____

_____

_____

_____

_____

_____

Suggested Prayer:

Dear Lord, I thank You for dying for me, and for giving me hope of eternity in Heaven with You! I love You and thank You for loving me...

The Single Mom Journey

The Single Mom Journey
Day 6

Talking To God

"The effectual fervent prayer of a righteous man availeth much." James 5:16b

As a single mom we are always trying to be the problem solver. If something needs fixed we try to figure out how to get it fixed. If our children need help with something we try to provide the solution. Sometimes it feels is as if we are bombarded with multiple obstacles in our lives at one time. I remember telling the Lord I needed strength, guidance, wisdom, and grace. But, so many times after praying, I'd then try to find a solution myself. Looking back now, I know I did not always rely on God as I should have. He always took care of us as He promised in His word. The state of Pennsylvania requires that everyone get their car inspected on a yearly basis. One year when I needed my car inspected, it would not pass the inspection and as a result I was not able to drive it. So, there we were with no vehicle, no way to get around. I have to admit I was not a happy camper, but after prayer and fasting with a close friend of mine the Lord quickly provided for this need. He guided an individual to give us a car and even pay for the title transfer. Believe me; I know what it is like to be overwhelmed and to feel like God does not care. I want to tell you though that He does. He loves you and wants to have a relationship with you. There were many times, I felt like I had so much weight on my shoulders and all I had to do was give it to God! I challenge you to not try to always be the problem solver, but rather talk to God and allow Him to solve your problems.

-Connie

Challenge ~ Day 6

In today's age there are multiple resources for communication. We can email, chat, text, talk on the phone, communicate on social sites, and many other avenues. With all of these resources at our fingertips, there are times when we still may feel like we have no one to talk to. As a single mom you do not have that husband to share your thoughts, feelings, emotions, problems, and other life issues with, and this can at times be difficult. Do you ever just want someone to talk to? Why not talk to God? Talking to God is simple. You do not have to login, dial a number, or click send, but rather you just have to begin speaking to Him. He is always there, and He is always willing to listen to you. David is a great Biblical example of someone that continuously talked to God through the good and the bad times of life. The book of Psalms is filled with conversations that David had with God. These conversations reveal David's ups and downs in his life. Some Psalms are joyous and some are sad. The Bible shows us in I Samuel 13:14 and Acts 13:22 that David was a man after God's own heart. David loved to talk to God. David was not perfect, but he laid his burdens down at God's feet. What about you? Who do you talk to in the good and bad times? Who will you talk to in the times to come? James 5:16b tells us that *"The effectual fervent prayer of a righteous man availeth much."* This means that talking to God will bring into your life great gain. The next time you feel alone dial into a conversation with God through prayer and Bible study, you will be amazed at how quickly that loneliness turns to happiness!

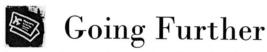 # Going Further

In one or two sentences describe what James 5:16b means to you?

How has James 5:16b helped you on your single mom journey?

Do you daily spend time in prayer? God is always available for you to talk to! Some people spend a block of time each day praying and others talk to God all day long. What are some ways that you could spend more time praying throughout the day? Try to begin implementing these ways into your daily schedule.

We often try to be the problem solvers, but we have to get in the practice of giving our problems to God. List 1-5 areas in your life that you need to give to God? Right now pray about these items, seeking God's help and guidance in them.

Write about an occasion in the past month that God answered one of your prayers? Were you happy with the outcome?   Sometimes God answers prayers but it is not the answer we were seeking. Regardless of His answer, did you thank Him for it?

Take Action

Write a note to God thanking Him for the things He has done and is doing in your life. Talk to Him about your burdens and problems. Look back at this note often and see what God has done in your life.

Prayer Time

Prayer Requests:

_____

_____

_____

_____

_____

_____

Suggested Prayer:

Dear Lord, I thank You for loving me, and giving me the ability to call upon You whenever I want. I ask that You would guide me as I begin to talk to You more. Please give me strength to get through my single mom struggles, realizing that You are always there to listen to me...

The Single Mom Journey

The Single Mom Journey
Day 7

<u>Overcoming Fear</u>

"For God hath not given us the spirit of fear; but of power, and of love, and of a sound mind."
II Timothy 1:7

Ever since I was a small child fear has overcome me easily. From the wooded area located behind our home to the basement inside our home I was scared. When I got older this fear of the unknown was replaced with a fear of reality. A few months after we got married I came to the realization that the man I had married was an abusive alcoholic. There were multiple occasions where he would go out and get completely drunk and when he was in this state of mind I never knew what he was going to do. My entire body would shake in fear when he was coming home. If you are wondering why I did not just leave this abusive man, well, he told me if I did he would find me and take our son away to be with him. Mainly the thought of losing my son kept me there but also my vow, "till death do us part." I was always thankful when he would just come home and pass out, because I knew for that night I would be safe. Then when my husband left the fear of the unknown returned. I would hear noises and be fearful that someone was breaking into our home. As a single mom I feared many situations: Would my children be ok? Was I being a good mother? Would I be able to provide? These questions filled with fear went on and on, and they continued for years. It was not until my children were out of the house that I came to the conclusion that I needed to rest in God's arms. It was not until then that this verse became real to me. I challenge you today that regardless of the situation you are in do not let fear control you as I did for too many years, but rest in the almighty arms of God.

-Connie

Challenge ~ Day 7

September 11, 2001 is a historic day for the United States. Many individuals remember exactly what they were doing when they heard of the events that were taking place. It shook our nation emotionally and spiritually. Many heroes came about from this historic day, due to their efforts of acting in time of need. One such man was named Todd Beamer. Todd boarded United Flight 93 going from Newark, NJ to San Francisco, CA. His flight was one of the planes that were hijacked that day by terrorists, and instead of going to San Francisco, as he had planned; his flight was being re-routed to Washington DC. Todd and a few other passengers on the plane knew that they had to do something. They could not just sit in their seats with fear and allow these terrorists to complete their mission. Todd's last audible words were "Are you guys ready? Let's roll." The group conquered fear and took over the plane, which soon came crashing down in a field in Somerset, Pennsylvania. Though none of the passengers on that flight survived that day, Todd became a national hero because he gave his life to save others.[5] They overcame their fear and conquered the obstacles that were set in front of them. II Timothy 1:7 shows us that fear is not from God. Fear limits us from living to our fullest potential. What are you fearful of? II Timothy 1:7 also shows us that God has given us power, love, and a sound mind. When you become fearful, remember that we have power through the Lord; trust Him today to help you overcome your fear.

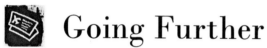 # Going Further

In one or two sentences describe what II Timothy 1:7 means to you?

How has II Timothy 1:7 helped you on your single mom journey?

What is something that you have not been able to accomplish in your life because of fear? For many individuals fear holds them back from reaching their potential in life.

In one sentence define fear.

Write a paragraph about someone (friend, family member, celebrity, Bible character, etc.) who could not overcome fear and kept them from reaching their full potential. What were they fearful of or why did they struggle with fear? Why weren't they able to overcome it? What could they have done differently? What was the end result?

Write a paragraph about someone (friend, family member, celebrity, Bible character, etc.) who struggled with fear and overcame it. Why did they struggle with fear? How did they overcome it? What was the end result? What can you learn from their example?

Take Action

Write out a list of your fears. Begin meditating on II Timothy 1:7 daily thinking of your fears and asking God to help you conquer them.

Prayer Time

Prayer Requests:

_____

_____

_____

_____

_____

_____

Suggested Prayer:

Dear Lord, I realize only through You am I able to overcome my fears. I ask that from this day forward, You will strengthen me to live with power, love, and a sound mind...

The Single Mom Journey

The Single Mom Journey
Day 8

Dealing With Discouragement

"Cast thy burden upon the LORD, and he shall sustain thee: he shall never suffer the righteous to be moved." Psalm 55:22

When I was young, I had the same storybook dreams that most young girls have. The ones where we find prince charming, have a big elaborate wedding, and live happily ever after in a great big mansion. Please understand that I am not complaining about the way things turned out, but life did not exactly happen the way that I had imagined. I am guessing that maybe you have had a similar situation. You did not grow up wanting to be a single mom, but here you are. Have you felt any discouragement during your single mom journey? If you have don't worry, it is completely normal. You are trying to conquer one of the hardest obstacles you will ever face in your life. I constantly dealt with discouragement along my journey. Single parenting and discouragement go hand-in-hand. I was often discouraged knowing that the dream of being a stay at home mom would never come to fruition. I was often discouraged because I was not able to provide more for my children the way I wanted to. Then one day I finally realized that I needed to completely give my new life journey to God and He would lead the way. The verse that showed me this is found in Romans 8:28 *"And we know that all things work together for good to them that love God, to them who are the called according to his purpose."* No matter how hard your road is God will make a way. I challenge you to give your discouragement to God, because only through Him will you find true peace amidst the storms of life!

-Connie

Challenge ~ Day 8

As the sounds of marching, yelling, and chariots were drawing nigh, the fearfulness grew inside the Israelites. Would they be captive again or worse murdered? Suddenly, Moses lifted his rod toward the Heavens, trusting that God would save them, and the miracle of the parting of the Red Sea took place. The waters drew back providing a dry pathway to walk, and as soon as they were all across, the waters came tumbling down destroying the soldiers that sought destruction upon their lives. (Exodus 14). God had delivered them from their discouragement, and at the end of this trial, the Bible says, *"And Israel saw that great work which the LORD did upon the Egyptians: and the people feared the LORD, and believed the LORD, and his servant Moses."* Exodus 14:31. This is just one example of Moses casting burdens upon the Lord for himself and the Israelites during their journey through the wilderness to the Promised Land, and God miraculously delivered them. No matter the circumstances they faced, God sustained them! Psalm 55:22 tells us to *"Cast thy burden upon the LORD, and he shall sustain thee."* Only God is able to help us in every moment of our life. By allowing God to deal with your discouragement, you too shall be able to look back and see what great things He has done for you. Deal with your discouragement by giving it to God today!

 # Going Further

In one or two sentences describe what Psalm 55:22 means to you?

How has Psalm 55:22 helped you on your single mom journey?

In your own words define discouragement?

In the note from Connie she stated that Romans 8:28 helped in her discouraging times. Find a verse that will help you when you are discouraged. Write it out below and begin memorizing it so that you can quote it when needed.

Write down some great things that God has done in your life over the past year. Now take some time and thank the Lord!

Have you given your single mom journey to God? Sometimes it is something to be done on a daily basis? If you have given it to God then write a note to Him thanking Him for what He has done for you! If you have not given it to God then write a note asking Him for strength in the good and bad times.

Take Action

Make a list of the items you are currently discouraged about in your life. Pray over them and then begin praying over them for the next 22 days that God would deliver you from them.

Prayer Time

Prayer Requests:

_____

_____

_____

_____

_____

_____

Suggested Prayer:

Dear Lord, I give You my burdens. I ask that in this time of discouragement in my life that You would sustain me. I trust You and love You...

The Single Mom Journey

The Single Mom Journey
Day 9

<u>Trusting God</u>

"Trust in the LORD with all thine heart; and lean not unto thine own understanding. In all thy ways acknowledge him, and he shall direct thy paths." Proverbs 3:5-6

Well, we are finally here. Today is the last day of preparation and tomorrow begins week 1 of our trip. I challenge you to keep moving on a successful path in your single mom journey. There are so many moms all around us that have given up. You cannot afford to face the consequences for giving up along this journey. No matter how hard it is do not give up. Keep moving forward; you will not regret it! As a single mom hard times often come, but whether they are monetary, emotional, physical, or any other obstacle trusting God is the only way to get through. I understand what it is like to not have any food, to receive utility shut off notices, to almost be evicted, to not have any money for gas, and other such scenarios; but God always brought us through. Trusting God is something that all of us have to decide on a daily basis. When these hard times hit I challenge you to keep looking up, because the Lord will provide if you just trust in Him.

-Connie

Challenge ~ Day 9

"Children whose parents separate are significantly more likely to engage in early sexual activity, abuse drugs, and experience conduct and mood disorders. This effect is especially strong for children whose parents separated when they were five or younger."[6] As a single mom not only do you have to go at it alone, but the statistics are also heavily stacked against you and your family. If you search the internet for "fatherless statistics" or something similar, a plethora of similar statistics will appear. This is scary stuff, but there is hope. You and your family do not have to become one of the statistics. Nevertheless, as you travel along your single mom journey there will be victories and there will be losses, but Proverbs 3:5-6 gives us guidance on how we need to trust God in every life circumstance. In Daniel 6, we read of how Daniel, as a faithful servant and follower of God, was cast into a lion's den. The intention for this punishment was that he would be eaten and destroyed. Even though he had been following God consistently, God allowed Daniel to go through this trial. Even in the lion's den Daniel trusted God, and this was the result: *"My God hath sent his angel, and hath shut the lions' mouths, that they have not hurt me: forasmuch as before him innocency was found in me; and also before thee, O king, have I done no hurt."* Daniel 6:22. The world is like these lions, and it wants to destroy you and your family, but if you act as Daniel did and put your trust in God, He will help you! In the good times and the bad times, trust God with your life, for only He can protect you!

 # Going Further

In one or two sentences describe what Proverbs 3:5-6 means to you?

How has Proverbs 3:5-6 helped you on your single mom journey?

In your own words define trust?

Write a paragraph about someone (friend, family member, celebrity, Bible character, etc.) who struggled with trusting God with their life. Why did they struggle with trust? Why weren't they able to overcome it? What could they have done differently? What was the end result?

Write a paragraph about someone (friend, family member, celebrity, Bible character, etc.) who struggled with trust. Why did they struggle with trust? How did they overcome it? What was the end result? How can you learn from their example?

Take Action

Write out five areas in your life that you completely trust God and five areas where you struggle trusting Him. Write a letter to God thanking Him for helping you trust Him in certain areas and asking Him to help you trust Him in the areas where you struggle.

Prayer Time

Prayer Requests:

_____
_____
_____
_____
_____
_____

Suggested Prayer:

Dear Heavenly Father, please help me today to trust You with every aspect of my single mom journey. You have created me and I trust that You will guide me through any circumstance that I may face...

The Single Mom Journey

THE TRIP - WEEK 1

Days 10-16

The Single Mom Journey
Day 10

<u>Forgiveness</u>

"Let all bitterness, and wrath, and anger, and clamour, and evil speaking, be put away from you, with all malice: and be ye kind one to another, tenderhearted, forgiving one another, even as God for Christ's sake hath forgiven you."
Ephesians 4:31-32

I often quoted Ephesians 4:32 to my children, but it took me quite some time for *"forgiving one another"* to be a part of my own life. How could I forgive my husband for leaving me to raise three kids without any support? I heard a wonderful message on bitterness at my home church and my husband's brother, Pastor David Teis, wrote me a letter and advised me to never get bitter because it would destroy my kids and I. It was very easy to be bitter towards my husband and also even towards God. My husband's family and I had prayed for him to change and get right with God, but he never did. My dream of having the perfect family and being a stay-at-home wife and mother certainly was not coming true. It is true that bitterness makes you unhappy and irritable. I used to be a happy person, but I was now bitter and unhappy. In time with God's help I was able to forgive him. I saw my ex-husband fourteen years after he left and at that time I knew that I had forgiven him for all that he had done. I also asked God to forgive me for being bitter toward Him because it was not God's fault in any way. Since Satan wants the bitterness to weave its way back into my life, I have to daily give my life to God and allow Him to handle the past. At the end of verse 32 it says that God forgave us and since He forgives me for the multitude of wrong that I have done, how can I not forgive others?

–Connie

Challenge ~ Day 10

You cannot escape the reality that there are times when you must forgive people. Since no one is perfect people can bring hurt and disappointment. Forgiveness is a major step towards success along your single mom journey. You must forgive in order to continue on. This is the first day of your trip and today you must make a very crucial decision. You may be thinking to yourself that you have already forgiven the person or situation that got you into this single mom journey. Aside from that, you may need to forgive others as well. A lot of times there is bitterness and anger stored up that gets released. This bitterness and anger can be directed toward the person that directly hurt you, but it can also be towards your parents, siblings, co-workers, someone that has wronged or neglected you, someone that you may think caused your single mom experience, even anger towards God or towards someone that has not been mentioned. When forgiveness is ignored there are always consequences to pay. This consequence could be a broken relationship, a demolished future due to bitterness and anger, a lack of trust in other relationships, or many other things. When bitterness is planted in your life, it grows anger that is towards God. Many times, bitterness causes people to fight, hate, and even murder. Making this first step on your journey may be the hardest you will take. For some it may involve several steps, meaning that you have more than one person to forgive, but you need to start somewhere.

THE BASIS FOR FORGIVENESS: When Jesus died on the cross for you, He performed the ultimate act of forgiveness. He forgave you for every sin that you have or will ever commit (remember your responsibility is to accept this forgiveness – visit Day 1 for a review on His forgiveness). When Christ shed His blood on the cross it was for you to be forgiven of your sins. Just as Christ forgave you, you are responsible to forgive others. You are also responsible to ask forgiveness of any wrong doings that you do to others. In the Going Further section you must work through the 4 steps of forgiveness as you travel on the single mom journey, or you will not be able to successfully conquer this struggle in your life.

 # Going Further

In one or two sentences describe what Ephesians 4:31-32 means to you?

How has Ephesians 4:31-32 helped you on your single mom journey?

In one sentence define forgiveness.

You must take the following four steps on this part of the journey:

1. Forgive the person(s) that have caused you to be on this single mom journey. If your single mom journey started because of death, then make sure you are not bitter towards God for allowing this to happen. Is there anyone that you need to forgive that you think had any part in you starting your single mom journey?

2. Forgive yourself. Regardless of your past let it go and move on! Is there anything that you need to forgive yourself for that you think had any part in you starting your single mom journey?

3. Forgive others. Is there anyone in your life that you need to forgive, regardless of whether or not it has to do with your single mom journey?

4. Ask God for forgiveness. Have you been angry at God for anything? Ask God to forgive you for any areas where you have had anger or bitterness.

Take Action

Make a list of the individuals in your life that you need to forgive. Begin to pray for them and ask God to forgive you for any bitterness, hatred, or anger that you may feel. Then daily seek His strength and guidance to love those that have hurt you.

Prayer Time

Prayer Requests:

_____

_____

_____

_____

_____

_____

Suggested Prayer:

Dear Lord, please forgive me for not being forgiving to those who have hurt me or who have caused me pain. Please forgive me for my bitterness and anger, and please help me to forgive others and to put You first in my life...

The Single Mom Journey

The Single Mom Journey
Day 11

Inferiority

"Not that we are sufficient of ourselves to think any thing as of ourselves; but our sufficiency is of God." II Corinthians 3:5

When I was in the seventh grade, I was riding the bus home as we arrived at my stop I began to exit the bus, but just before I did an eighth grader looked at me and said a very rude comment regarding my appearance. Now sure, I was in seventh grade and I had acne and other "junior high syndromes" but even to this day I still remember the hurt this boy caused me to feel. From that moment, I began to feel as if everyone saw me that way. As I got older I grew out of those junior high looks and my self-confidence became more established. When my husband moved away those seventh grade feelings came back. I felt ugly and worthless. The man I had poured myself into for 10 years walked away from me. It wasn't until later that I realized I was not the reason that he left, but it was because of his own selfishness and sinful habits. There are different levels of inferiority, but most often inferiority comes from a lack of self-confidence. I started to gain ground on conquering inferiority after a friend referred me to a book about true inner beauty. The book showed how God created us and how we are all beautiful in His eyes. In addition, I was introduced to an incredible Bible verse in I Samuel 16:7 which says *"for the LORD seeth not as man seeth; for man looketh on the outward appearance, but the LORD looketh on the heart."* I challenge you to claim a Bible verse for any area that you may feel inferior. Also, remember that God cares about your inner beauty more than He cares about your outer beauty.

-Connie

Challenge ~ Day 11

When a woman has a dedicated husband and an active father for her children she has something special. A good husband and father is a support system, partner, friend, encourager, leader, and most importantly a faithful servant of God. A good husband is someone that loves you and your children and cares for every need that you have and strives to push you toward your greatest potential. A father teaches his children. Dads give their daughters security and their sons confidence and they provide protection, show encouragement, and give guidance on things such as: driving, dating, friendships, and much more. Since your children are fatherless, it is obvious that they do not have a dad to be these things for them. Whether their father has passed away or he simply lives down the street from them, there are still feelings of inferiority. Fellow mothers may tell you about an activity their children had with their husband or about something their husband taught their children, and this may make you feel inferior as a single mom. This is understandable and normal in your situation. Though this feeling may never disappear completely there are steps you can take to help your children on their fatherless journey. As a single mom, you may at times feel inferior to friends and family that possess a "complete" family unit because you desire to have a healthy environment for your children. You must fight these feelings of inferiority! Satan wants you to fail on this journey and inferiority is just another one of those weapons he will use to fight against you, but don't give up! Let's look at Jesus' life. He was given the most unusual job of all time. The ultimate reason for His earthly existence was for Him to die on a cross to save people from an eternal death in Hell when they die. What a task He was given and He gloriously fulfilled His calling! Not that you have been given a task that is anything compared to what Jesus went through, but you certainly have been given an unusual job. When God designed marriage, He meant it to be for a man and a woman, and He meant for children to have both parents. Since you are doing this alone, it may be discouraging at times and inferiority to others may arise, but keep pressing on! Many times your inferiority may be overwhelming, but if you continue trusting God with your inferiority you will be able to live a successful life. II Corinthians 3:5 says *"not that we are sufficient of ourselves to think anything as of ourselves; but our sufficiency is of God."*

Going Further

In one or two sentences describe what II Corinthians 3:5 means to you?

How has II Corinthians 3:5 helped you on your single mom journey?

In one sentence define inferiority.

What are some positive steps you could begin to take to help you overcome your inferiority?

Write out 2-5 circumstances where you have felt inferior to others as a single mom and then describe how you overcame them.

Take Action

Make a list of the areas in your life that make you feel inferior to others. Then begin to pray daily that God will help you overcome your inferiority.

Prayer Time

Prayer Requests:

_____

_____

_____

_____

_____

_____

Suggested Prayer:

Dear Lord, I give my inferiority to You. I trust You for You have made me and my sufficiency is from You. I thank You for being my Confidence and my Strength...

The Single Mom Journey

The Single Mom Journey
Day 12

Outcast

"And God heard the voice of the lad; and the angel of God called to Hagar out of heaven, and said unto her, What aileth thee, Hagar? fear not; for God hath heard the voice of the lad where he is. Arise, lift up the lad, and hold him in thine hand; for I will make him a great nation."
Genesis 21:17-18

When I got divorce papers in the mail I was devastated. Those papers made it so final, and since my husband lived in Nevada he could divorce me without my consent. When I got married I planned on it being "till death do us part." My church was not prepared to handle single parent families; I often felt looked down upon for my divorce or for being a single mom. Please understand my Pastor and his wife and other church staff did not look down on me but rather some of the fellow members in the church. In their eyes, I was beneath them. I would find out about parties and events people had that were only for couples and their children but not for single parents and their children. I truly think it was easier for people to avoid being around an uncomfortable situation than to have to deal with it. There were people who took the avoidance route but maybe because they only saw me as a sinner and a hurting single mom. The feeling of being an outcast is directly from Satan. He wants you to feel like nobody cares about you not even the Church, but this is not the case. As I began to work through this I realized that many people did care and then I was able to build relationships with them. After I got over the feeling of being an outcast and allowed that to be my attitude, I realized that it was not that I was actually an outcast but rather that Satan wanted me to feel like an outcast. There is a big difference in feeling as an outcast and actually being an outcast. I challenge you to realize that feeling as an outcast is the Devil striving to destroy your faith. Instead of getting down give it to God!

–Connie

Challenge ~ Day 12

As a single mom you have probably felt like an outcast at one point or another. Regardless of who made you feel this way, you must overcome these feelings to conquer your single mom journey. You and your children are precious to God. In Genesis 21 the Bible tells us that Hagar, Abrahams bondwoman (or slave), and Ishmael, the son that Abraham had with Hagar, were sent away from the safety and comfort of their home to dwell in the wilderness with just some bread and a bottle of water. Abraham was pressured by his wife Sarah to send them away, and he submitted to the pressure not caring what may happen to Hagar and his own flesh and blood, Ishmael. This is the way that you may feel at times, like an outcast, as if no one cares about you and your children. When these feelings arise, you must remember that you are special to God and He care about you. When you begin to doubt God or feel like an outcast read Genesis 21, because we not only see Hagar and Ishmael being rejected by Abraham but we also see them being accepted and protected by God. Genesis 21:15-16 shows us that when the bottle of water was gone, Hagar knew that they could not survive so she cast her son into the bushes and continued on her journey and when she was at a good distance from him she said *"Let me not see the death of the child"* and then she began to weep. Hagar was not only an outcast but now she was destitute, with no hope, but then God came through, as He does when we put our trust in Him and it says *"And God heard the voice of the lad; and the angel of God called to Hagar out of heaven, and said unto her, What aileth thee, Hagar? fear not; for God hath heard the voice of the lad where he is. Arise, lift up the lad, and hold him in thine hand; for I will make him a great nation. And God opened her eyes, and she saw a well of water; and she went, and filled the bottle with water, and gave the lad drink. And God was with the lad; and he grew, and dwelt in the wilderness, and became an archer."* We see here that God came through big for Hagar and Ishmael, and He will do the same for you if you rely on Him. The next time you are feeling like an outcast and ready to give up seek the Lord, because He cares about you!

 # Going Further

Read Geneses 21.

In a paragraph describe what Genesis 21 means to you?

In one sentence define outcast.

How has Genesis 21 helped you on your single mom journey?

 # Take Action

Who or what makes you feel like an outcast? You do not need to feel this way. Make a list of who (use initials or create a nickname that only you would recognize) or what makes you feel this and begin praying about how to overcome these feelings. Sometimes there are relationships you need to reconcile or even break or sometimes there are feelings or thoughts that you need to overcome in order to not allow those feelings to overwhelm you. Do whatever is needed until all of these feelings are gone!

Prayer Time

Prayer Requests:

_____

_____

_____

_____

_____

_____

Suggested Prayer:

Dear God, thank You for caring about me and my children as much as You cared for Hagar and Ishmael. Help me to rely solely on You as I strive to conquer this journey...

The Single Mom Journey

The Single Mom Journey
Day 13

Envy

"Thou shalt not covet thy neighbour's house, thou shalt not covet thy neighbour's wife, nor his manservant, nor his maidservant, nor his ox, nor his ass, nor any thing that is thy neighbour's." Exodus 20:17

Wow! There are probably very few people who have not struggled with envy or jealousy. I of course envied women who had a good husband, especially those who helped with the children. I envied those who had a nice house and a nice car. I envied stay at home moms, because I really wanted to be one. This list could go on and on. Through a lot of prayer I learned to be content. Today, I still sometimes have to ask God to forgive me of my envy. After I learned contentment I realized God had blessed me with three fabulous children. My children are now grown and happily married with families of their own, and this is something that money cannot buy. Having a close relationship with my children and grandchildren helps me to be thankful for what God has given me instead of being envious of what I don't have. Through this I have learned that I need to be truly happy where God has placed me today instead of looking at others with envy. I also realized later in life that many of the people that I envied were not as happy as they had appeared. I challenge you to not let envy get in your way on your single mom journey, because it can be a big road block that could hold you back!

-Connie

Challenge ~ Day 13

Who do you envy? What makes you jealous? What do you covet? Why? These are questions that you must ask yourself and then work at overcoming them. Covetousness is sin. Luke 15:11 is the beginning of the Parable of the Lost Son or Prodigal Son. If you have never heard this story before, please read Luke 15:11-32. It is about a young man that desires to have his inheritance early so that he can go out and live the "good life." He wanted to party and that is what he did; he went out and after many foolish decisions, he lost all of the inheritance that he had. You see, his father divided his estate in half and the son had quickly gone through all of this money. After the money was gone, the son found himself eating with the swine out of desperation and this forced him to go back to his father and ask for forgiveness with the thought that his father might allow him to become one of his servants. When he returned to his father's house we are told that his father restored him to the status of a son and even went to the point to kill a fatted calf for a coming home party. But this is not the part of the story that we want to focus on, fast forward to verse 28 and it shows us that his brother, the one that stayed home and continued in the work of his father's house, became angry. He was angered that they would kill the fatted calf on behalf of his wayward brother. He was jealous that his father never allowed him to kill a fatted calf and have a party. He simply envied his brother. In verses 31-32, it shows us that everything that remained at the father's house was the sons and his father instructs him to be glad because: *"and be glad: for this thy brother was dead, and is alive again; and was lost, and is found."* This brother had to learn to not envy his brother. Envy is something that will hinder you and your relationships. Let it go today. Rejoice in the success of others. Our theme verse today says not to covet: *"any thing that is thy neighbour's."* Thank God for what He has given to you and give up the action of jealousy today!

 # Going Further

Read Luke 15:11-32.

In one or two sentences describe what Luke 15:11-32 means to you?

How has Luke 15:11-32 helped you on your single mom journey?

In one or two sentences describe what Exodus 20:17 means to you?

82

How has Exodus 20:17 helped you on your single mom journey?

In one sentence define envy.

Write a paragraph about someone (friend, family member, celebrity, Bible character, etc.) who could not overcome envy and it kept them from reaching their full potential. What or who did they envy? Why weren't they able to overcome it? What could they have done differently? What was the end result?

Write a paragraph about someone (friend, family member, celebrity, Bible character, etc.) who struggled with envy and overcame it. Why did they struggle with envy? How did they overcome it? What was the end result? How can you learn from them?

Take Action

Draw two columns: 1. What you envy, 2. What God has blessed you with and begin filling in these columns. Then begin praying and asking God to help you overcome the envy, jealousy, and covetousness in your life; and thank Him for the blessings He has provided.

Prayer Time

Prayer Requests:

_____
_____
_____
_____
_____
_____

Suggested Prayer:

Dear Lord, I realize that You do not want me to envy, covet, or be jealous of anyone or anything; please help me as I strive to overcome these feelings in my life...

The Single Mom Journey

The Single Mom Journey
Day 14

<u>Giving It All To God</u>

"Be still, and know that I am God: I will be exalted among the heathen, I will be exalted in the earth." Psalm 46:10

I look back now and realize that I spent a lot of time trying to figure out how I was going to take care of everything by myself. My mind was continually running from one topic to another, trying to figure out how to make this single mom journey easier. The entire time I was worrying, God was in control. In a previous entry, I mentioned that after my husband left we had to move in with my parents, but after a short stint with them we had the ability to move into a rental home of our own. My uncle had found an affordable home for us that was right across the street from where I had worked. This was such a blessing, because now we could be a family in our own home again. This home was not desirable: it was filled with mice, the furnace did not work (after an entire winter we found this out), there was a rat colony outside because of trash that was left behind, and my children and I shared one bedroom, but aside from all of its issues it was still our home. I believe God gave us this home to get us back on our feet again and I took pride in it regardless of its faults. And eventually the mice and rats were gone and the furnace got fixed. As I look back this is just one example of the multitude of blessings that God poured out on my family because I decided to give this journey to Him. I challenge you today to give your entire single mom experience to God, because He will bless you for it!

–Connie

Challenge ~ Day 14

On day 1 you were presented with Salvation and giving your heart to Jesus. Day 9 you learned about trusting God and today is about giving your life to God. Please read Romans 14:7-9. This passage shows us that *"we are the Lord's."* If you surrender to His perfect will for your life it will be a lot easier than if you tried to go on your own life path. In Revelations 3:15-16 it says: *"I know thy works, that thou art neither cold nor hot: I would thou wert cold or hot. So then because thou art lukewarm, and neither cold nor hot, I will spue thee out of my mouth."* These two verses show that we as humans are either for Christ (hot) or against Christ (cold). It is better for us to be upfront about being cold or hot than to be partially for Christ and partially for the world (lukewarm). As Christians we must be on fire for Christ, there is no room nor is there any time for us to be lukewarm, and there is a punishment for this type of behavior. Being a lukewarm Christian makes Christ want to vomit. Now you have three choices that you have to choose from: do you want to be cold and reject Christ, do you want to be lukewarm and make Christ vomit, or do you want to be hot and serve Christ in every area of your life? There are a multitude of examples in the Bible, throughout history, and even around you today where individuals either gave their life to God or they did not, and you and I get to learn from their examples. A famous preacher once said, *"He must be Lord of all to be Lord at all."*[7] Give your life to God today and surrender to His ultimate plan for your life.

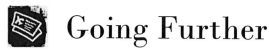 # Going Further

Read Romans 14:7-9.

In one or two sentences describe what Romans 14:7-9 means to you?

How has Romans 14:7-9 helped you on your single mom journey?

In one or two sentences describe what Psalm 46:10 means to you?

How has Psalm 46:10 helped you on your single mom journey?

What are 2-5 things in your life that you have given to God? How did it feel to hand it over to Him? What was the end result?

 # Take Action

Write out a letter to God telling Him the things in your life that you need and want to surrender to Him. Be specific. Pray for those things that you have a hard time letting go of. Tell Him you give Him your single mom journey and really mean it.

Prayer Time

Prayer Requests:

_____

_____

_____

_____

_____

_____

Suggested Prayer:

Dear Lord, I realize that in order for You to be Lord at all, You need to be Lord of all areas of my life. You are my Master and Creator and I give You every aspect of my life today. Thank You for constantly giving me guidance and I ask for Your strength along the rest of my journey...

The Single Mom Journey

The Single Mom Journey
Day 15

Mistakes

"Brethren, I count not myself to have apprehended: but this one thing I do, forgetting those things which are behind, and reaching forth unto those things which are before, I press toward the mark for the prize of the high calling of God in Christ Jesus." Philippians 3:13-14

I have made my share of mistakes and even after allowing God to be my all there was a point where I took my eyes off of Him to pursue my own fleshly wants and desires. I got into a relationship with a man that was unhealthy for my children and myself. I had been looking for comfort from a man and I felt as though I just had to have someone, but after this huge mistake I realized that I was completely wrong. You would think after being in such a bad situation with my husband that I would have known better, but when you take your eyes off of God and pursue your own wants and desires you will fall. I fell, I admit it, and I regret it. This mistake of mine hurt my children and even for a time my relationship with my children. After some time, I finally realized that I was making a mistake and began to strive to repair what damage I had caused. This was a mistake and I wish I could go back in time and fix what happened, but I cannot. Sometimes when you make a mistake the results remain for years and I have seen this in my own life. I challenge you to keep your eyes focused on God along your single mom journey, so not to make the same mistakes I did. Forget about your own fleshly desires and be filled with the desire to fulfill God's will for your life. You will not regret it, I can promise you that.

-Connie

Challenge ~ Day 15

Everyone makes mistakes, some are big and some are small, but everyone has a past and how one handles their past failures is one of the hardest parts of life. Andre Agassi was arguably one of the best male tennis players of all time and perhaps the most well-known tennis player of his time. The list goes on and on of all the championships and awards that he won during his career. Agassi started his professional career at age 16 where he had much success, but then about seven years later he began having trouble with his wrist and it required him to have surgery in 1993. Two years later he reached the world's number one ranking for the first time in his career. This world ranking lasted only about 6 months and then his wrist injury resurfaced; his life began to take a downward path due to poor choices. In 1997 Andre Agassi admitted to using crystal methamphetamine after failing a drug test. This lack of judgment could have ruined Agassi and the career that he strived so hard to build, but instead of continuing on with these poor choices he decided to get his life back on track. He decided to put these mistakes in his past and began working hard to get back to the professional tennis player status that he once held. Agassi went on to be number one in the world once again by the end of 1999.[8] This man could have continued on in his self-pity, his drug usages, and other life altering habits, but he decided to let go of the past and look to the future. Today's theme verses from Philippians 3 are a great example of how we must handle the mistakes of our past. They show us to forget the past (good or bad), focus on the future, and press on. Regardless of your past failures, let them go. That is right; let them go; forget about them; do not let them affect your future any longer; move on with your new life of serving God with all of your heart, soul, and mind. Reach to the future and press on with all of your might! Your past is your past; begin today reaching to the future, and make sure that your future is centered around living for God!

 # Going Further

In one or two sentences describe what Philippians 3:13-14 means to you?

How has Philippians 3:13-14 helped you on your single mom journey?

When you think of your future what do you picture? Everyone has dreams; start chasing those dreams today! In the following time frames write out what you think your life will be like at that time:

1 YEAR FROM NOW:

5 YEARS FROM NOW:

10 YEARS FROM NOW:

20 YEARS FROM NOW:

Now, write an action plan on how to achieve these dreams. What steps will it take to achieve these plans? What do you need to overcome or accomplish to attain them? Make sure that your relationship with God is the center of your action plan.

Take Action

Make a list of your top 3-5 life mistakes, you do not have to be specific, just give them a name, but be sure to write them down. Have you overcome them? If not, what is it going to take for you to overcome these mistakes? Do you need to ask for forgiveness from God or others, do you need to let go of some bitterness that you have been holding onto, or do you need to simply just quit dwelling on the past? Whatever is holding you back from dealing with the issues on your list make every effort possible to let them go.

Prayer Time

Prayer Requests:

_____

_____

_____

_____

_____

_____

Suggested Prayer:

Dear God, please forgive me for the mistakes of my past. Please help me to forget my past, reach to the future, and press on in my relationship with You and the life that You have given to me. Thank You for being a forgiving God and loving me despite my shortcomings...

The Single Mom Journey

The Single Mom Journey

Day 16

Purity Of Mind And Heart

"Flee also youthful lusts: but follow righteousness, faith, charity, peace, with them that call on the Lord out of a pure heart." II Timothy 2:22

It's very important to watch clean shows on TV and read clean books, because your mind can become easily corrupted. The most overlooked type of sin is that of what is in the media. We are daily surrounded with TV shows, movies, and music that tell us that adultery, swearing, being unkind to others (including murder), etc. are okay and have no consequences. We are constantly taught to be self-centered, thinking that our needs are the only thing that should matter to us. Unfortunately, these messages are only getting worse. We must realize that these things are absolutely not acceptable to God, and we must separate ourselves from them. Being the head of the household you must set some standards for your home. As single moms our guard must be up, because Satan wants to destroy us and our families! In I Peter 5:8 it says, *"Be sober, be vigilant; because your adversary the devil, as a roaring lion, walketh about, seeking whom he may devour."* Please don't fret though, because the verse before that takes away those worries and fear of this roaring lion where it says, *"casting all your care upon him; for he careth for you."* God truly does care about you and your family. He wants you to be pure and He wants to protect you from the destruction that the devil can and will cause your family if you don't trust in the Lord! I challenge you today to keep your heart and mind pure on your single mom journey...your children are counting on you!

–Connie

Challenge ~ Day 16

A converted Indian once said the following *"I have two dogs living in me - a mean dog and a good dog. They are always fighting. The mean dog wants me to do bad things, and the good dog wants me to do good things. Do you want to know which dog wins? The one I feed the most!"*[9] This statement holds true to all Christians: past, present, and future. Just because you are a Christian does not mean that it is easy to be pure, and in fact, sometimes it is harder, because we are often geared to want something even more when we know that we cannot have it. We must establish a priority of living pure in our lives this will ensure that we are feeding the good dog. Philippians 4:8 says, *"Finally, brethren, whatsoever things are true, whatsoever things are honest, whatsoever things are just, whatsoever things are pure, whatsoever things are lovely, whatsoever things are of good report; if there be any virtue, and if there be any praise, think on these things."* If you fill your life daily with pure things such as: Scripture, prayer, good friends, wise counsel, a good attitude, etc. and avoid things of the world such as: impure shows on TV, bad relationships, poor counsel, lack of prayer and devotions, etc. it will bring more happiness to your life. A good ending to add to the converted Indians story would be the following: if I continue to feed the bad dog and not the good, it will lead me down a path of destruction filled with regrets, but if I continue to feed the good dog and not the bad, it will lead me down a path of happiness filled with no regrets. Which dog will you continue to feed? If you have been feeding the bad dog, it is never too late to turn around and begin feeding the good. Feed the good dog today!

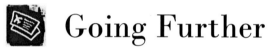 # Going Further

In one or two sentences describe what II Timothy 2:22 means to you?

How has II Timothy 2:22 helped you on your single mom journey?

In one sentence define what it means to be pure with your mind and heart.

God wants us to have the priority of purity in our lives. This includes being pure with inlets and outlets of your head: eyes, ears, mind, and mouth. What you let come in and exit out of these areas shows how pure your heart and mind are. Next to the categories below list 5 items that you need to abstain from and 5 items that you could replace them with. For example under ears you could list 5 songs that you listen to that the lyrics do not honor God, then list 5 songs that you could replace them with that do honor God.

EYES – What shouldn't you look at?	What could you replace it with?

EARS – What shouldn't you listen to?	What could you replace it with?

MIND – What shouldn't you think about?	What could you replace it with?

MOUTH – What shouldn't you say?	What could you replace it with?

Take Action

Make two lists, the first with ways you have been feeding the bad dog in your life, and the second with ways that you have been feeding the good dog in your life. Which dog is being fed more? Begin praying asking God to help you to only feed the good dog, eventually causing the bad dog to disappear!

Prayer Time

Prayer Requests:

_____

_____

_____

_____

_____

_____

Suggested Prayer:
Dear Lord, please help me to have the priority of purity in my daily life...

The Single Mom Journey

THE TRIP - WEEK 2

Days 17-23

The Single Mom Journey
Day 17

Purity Of Body

"But fornication, and all uncleanness, or covetousness, let it not be once named among you, as becometh saints; neither filthiness, nor foolish talking, nor jesting, which are not convenient: but rather giving of thanks." Ephesians 5:3-4

As a single mom there will most likely be times where you will desire a relationship with a man. I am not going to tell you whether or not you should date or even remarry, but what I will say is guard yourself! Guard your heart! Guard your children! And most importantly guard your relationship with God! Guard these things and do not let any man come between them or destroy them. As women we often desire that companionship with a man, but many times as a single mom these relationships with men will ruin our relationship with God and with our children. If the man you are with is affecting your relationship with God or your children - run! Run from that man, because he is not worth it! Do not sacrifice your future or your children's future on the altar of the immediate! I am speaking from experience. As I said before, I was in a relationship with a man that hindered my relationship with my children and with God and even until today I still see the consequences for this foolish decision. I allowed my fleshly desires and my feelings of wanting a man get in the way of what mattered most. I now am warning single moms not to fall into this trap like I did! When I finally woke up and realized the errors of my ways I ran for the hills and I challenge you to do the same! If you are in a healthy relationship that is honoring and pleasing to God then good for you, but if you are not pleasing Him learn from my mistake and move forward with your life - leave that relationship behind! I challenge you today to strive to flee from all tempting situations and pray hard that God will help protect you! Remind yourself constantly of the love, fulfillment, and forgiveness that comes only from our God, because your children deserve it and it will honor God!

-Connie

Challenge ~ Day 17

In today's society there are a variety of false statements being taught as truth. As Christians we need clarification on these lies to better understand how we can live pure with our body. If you were impure with your body in the past or were involved with any of the items listed below please understand that God is a forgiving God and He wants nothing more than for you to heal from the past and move forward with your future. Philippians 3:13-14 says *"Brethren, I count not myself to have apprehended: but this one thing I do, forgetting those things which are behind, and reaching forth unto those things which are before, I press toward the mark for the prize of the high calling of God in Christ Jesus."* If you are currently living against what the Bible teaches below, please understand that this list is not condemning you but rather preparing you for better choices in the future. God loves you and He wants you to turn from your sinful ways and follow Him. If you need some additional guidance on turning your life around please contact Life Factors Ministries at info@lifefactors.org. The following are some of the lies that our society teaches but with correct answers right beside them:

1. **Sex Outside of Marriage is Okay – FALSE**, the Bible says that sex outside of marriage is sin. In Ephesians 5:3 and several other passages, it clearly tells us that sex, fornication, or whatever you want to call it is wrong when not in the bonds of marriage, and this passage goes as far as to say that it should *"not be once named among you."* (See also I Corinthians 6:9-10; I Thessalonians 4:3-5; Hebrews 13:4)

2. **Homosexuality is Okay – FALSE**, the Bible says in several places that homosexuality is sin. In Jude 7 it says that Sodom and Gomorrha were destroyed because of fornication and homosexuality. (See also I Corinthians 6:9-10; Deuteronomy 23:17; Leviticus 18:22; Genesis 19:1-29; Ephesians 5:22-32; Romans 1:24-32)

3. **Abortion is Okay – FALSE**, in Exodus 20:13 the Bible says *"Thou shalt not kill."* Look up the word abort in a thesaurus and it is the subtle word for *"break off, call it quits, call off, cut off, drop, end, halt, interrupt, nullify, scrap, scratch, terminate"*[10] etc. Regardless of what you call it, abortion is the killing of an unborn baby, and murder is sin. (See also Ephesians 5:10-17; Galatians 5:19-21; Genesis 25:22-24; Luke 1:15; Luke 1:41-44; Ecclesiastes 11:5; Psalm 22:10)

4. **Immodesty is Okay – FALSE**, the Bible says in I Timothy 2:9 that *"women adorn themselves in modest apparel"* this is a command. As a Christian woman, you should wear clothes that are not revealing to men, and with every garment you buy ask yourself if it is honoring to the Lord for you to wear it. (See also Proverbs 11:22; Romans 14:13)

5. **In these statements we are not pushing the traditions of men, but striving to educate you on what the Bible truly teaches. Please find more help on purity at lifefactors.org.**

 # Going Further

In one or two sentences describe what Ephesians 5:3-4 means to you?

How has Ephesians 5:3-4 helped you on your single mom journey?

In one sentence define what it means to be pure with your body.

What are some ways that you could better guard your heart?

What are some ways that you could better guard your children's hearts?

What are your thoughts on what was said about marriage in the challenge? Are your thoughts Biblical? Look up I Corinthians 6:9-10, I Thessalonians 4:3-5, and Hebrews 13:4 and then write a summary in your own words on what Biblical marriage really is.

What are your thoughts on what was said about homosexuality in the Challenge? Are your thoughts Biblical? Look up I Corinthians 6:9-10, Deuteronomy 23:17, Leviticus 18:22, Genesis 19:1-29, Ephesians 5:22-32, and Romans 1:24-32 and then write a summary in your own words on what the Bible teaches about homosexuality.

What are your thoughts on what was said about abortion in the Challenge? Are your thoughts Biblical? Look up Ephesians 5:10-17, Galatians 5:19-21, Genesis 25:22-24, Luke 1:15, Luke 1:41-44, Ecclesiastes 11:5, Psalm 22:10, and Exodus 20:13 and then write a summary in your own words on what the Bible teaches about abortion.

What are your thoughts on what was said about immodesty in the Challenge? Are your thoughts Biblical? Look up Proverbs 11:22, Romans 14:13, and I Timothy 2:9 and then write a summary in your own words on what the Bible teaches about immodesty.

 # Take Action

Make a list of ways that you personally could live purer with your body, some examples would be pure talk, pure dress, pure thoughts, etc., and then begin striving to live them out today!

Prayer Time

Prayer Requests:

_____
_____
_____
_____
_____
_____

Suggested Prayer:
Dear Lord, I realize that my body is not mine, but rather a temple of the Holy Ghost, please help me to live pure every day...

The Single Mom Journey

Day 18

Unselfish

"Let nothing be done through strife or vainglory; but in lowliness of mind let each esteem other better than themselves. Look not every man on his own things, but every man also on the things of others." Philippians 2:3-4

Everyone is invited to a special party! Aren't you excited! This party is going to be centered on me, where we will not look at anyone but me and where we will do only what I want to do. This party will last for a period of 18-25 years and remember it is all about me! Sounds like a fun time doesn't it? You are probably thinking to yourself how awful this sounds and how terrible of me to be so selfish, but this is what it looks like when we are consumed with selfishness. You have to learn to focus on God and then others and then yourself. So many times the order is reversed and when it is our lives will be out of order. Selfishness = disorder and unselfishness = order. At a young age I started sending birthday cards to relatives and friends. This then turned into mailing out Christmas cards as well. At the beginning of my single mom journey God showed me that I needed to put others before myself. I began realizing that I was not the only one out there that had problems or was hurting. In fact, I realized that everyone could use some encouragement. From this point on I started sending not only birthday and Christmas cards but now I was sending sympathy, get well, encouragement, and other similar cards to friends, family, and acquaintances. My ministry of sending cards has helped me tremendously toward living with an unselfish attitude. I am not saying that you should start sending greeting cards, but strive to find something you are good at to help you put others first (cooking meals phone calls, visits, etc.) God wants you to do this because the Bible says *"let each esteem other better than themselves."*

-Connie

Challenge ~ Day 18

Your life should have the following order: God, others, and yourself. Think about your own life. Is it following this order? If it is then great! Keep going! But if it is out of order then it is time for a reality check. There is an old saying: "Hindsight sees 20/20," which basically means that if you would have known the consequences or rewards of something you did before you did it, you may have changed your actions. Jonah is a famous Bible character from the Old Testament that ultimately displays the meaning of this old saying. Jonah was told by God that he was to go to Nineveh but due to his hatred towards the people of Nineveh he ran from God. Jonah was a man with his priorities out of order. He was very selfish and much of which was driven by pride and bigotry or what some would call downright hatred. Jonah's life was not in order: God, others, and himself but rather himself first then God and others last. The consequences for Jonah not climbing his mountain were tremendous; he was swallowed by a great fish. He should be in the <u>Guinness Book of World Records</u> for being the only person to ever be inside a great fish's belly and live to tell about it. If Jonah would have had hindsight he would have never tried to run from God and it is certain that he would have quickly changed his priorities to God, others, and then himself. Being inside the great fish's belly and then being thrown up by the great fish was not a glamorous experience. Once Jonah saw that the only option was to serve the Lord by putting God's will first and also caring for others over himself he began to walk in God's steps. His life was quickly used by God to reach individuals. Ephesians 5:14-17 shows us that we must redeem the time that God has given to us. We must live a life that has God first, others second, and ourselves last. Do not give up on this journey for the consequences are too great!

 # Going Further

In one or two sentences describe what Philippians 2:3-4 means to you?

How has Philippians 2:3-4 helped you on your single mom journey?

In one sentence define selfishness.

Most everyone struggles with selfishness and often the reason for this selfishness is rooted on our inside? The challenge showed that Jonah's selfishness was driven by pride and bigotry or what some would call downright hatred. What drives you to selfishness in your own life?

Write a paragraph about someone (friend, family member, celebrity, Bible character, etc.) who could not overcome selfishness and it kept them from reaching their full potential. Why were they selfish? Why weren't they able to overcome it? What could they have done differently? What was the end result?

Write a paragraph about someone (friend, family member, celebrity, Bible character, etc.) that struggled with selfishness and overcame it. Why did they struggle with selfishness? How did they overcome it? What was the end result? How can you learn from their example?

Take Action

Make three columns and on the first column title it God, on the second column title it others, and on the third column title it myself. Under each heading write 5 areas of your life that you could improve in putting God first, others second, and yourself last.

Prayer Time

Prayer Requests:

_____
_____
_____
_____
_____
_____

Suggested Prayer:

Dear Lord, please forgive me for being selfish in any area of my life. Help me where my priorities have not been completely focused on putting You first, others second, and myself last. Please help me to keep my priorities straight from this day forward...

The Single Mom Journey

The Single Mom Journey
Day 19

<u>Thankfulness</u>

"Enter into his gates with thanksgiving, and into his courts with praise: be thankful unto him, and bless his name." Psalm 100:4

THANK YOU, THANK YOU, THANK YOU!!! Thank you to God for giving me three wonderful children and making me a mom! Thank you God for the family that I married into, because through them I heard about Jesus and was able to trust Him as my personal Savior! And thank you God for getting our family through the broken home journey! After looking back on this journey I am truly thankful, but I am not saying that it is always easy to be grateful for your life, but God wants to hear our thankfulness. Being a single mom is not always an easy road to travel, but if you trust in God then He will bring you through it! Our family struggled financially, but the blessings from God far outweighed this difficulty. One time when I was recovering from arm surgery and we were waiting for workers compensation benefits to start, times became very difficult. I did not know what we were going to do. I was not even sure where the groceries were going to come from, but then a very close friend of mine had a family member drop off an envelope with $50 in it. This amount may seem very small today, but I was able to buy groceries and pay on a bill with this money. On another occasion I had a desire to take my family to church on a Sunday night, but I knew that we did not have much gasoline. I asked God to provide the money for us to buy gasoline so we could get home. After church one of the Pastors came up and handed me $20 and said that he felt God wanted him to give it to us. Back then this was enough for an entire tank of gasoline in our car. These are just two examples of the many times that God provided for our family. I say all of this to say that God will provide and when He does be thankful! God will take care of you on this single mom journey as long as you trust Him through it!

–Connie

Challenge ~ Day 19

In 1621, the Plymouth colonists and Wampanoag Indians shared an autumn harvest feast that is acknowledged as one of the first Thanksgiving celebrations in the colonies. For more than two centuries, days of thanksgiving were celebrated by individual colonies and states. It wasn't until 1863, in the midst of the Civil War, that President Abraham Lincoln proclaimed a national Thanksgiving Day to be held each November.[11] Thanksgiving has truly come a long way since the first celebration. Thanksgiving is an amazing holiday, filled with family, fun, football, food, and whatever other comforting words that may come to your mind. It is a time of reflecting on the previous month, year, or several years acknowledging what God has done and how He has blessed and guided along your life journey. Whether or not you have a lot or a little there is always something to be thankful for. An amazing cure for hurt is thankfulness. When things of this life have you down think about all of the ways God has blessed in the past and how He is currently blessing. Thank God for who He is and what He has done. Be thankful for Him being Omniscient (all knowing), Omnipresent (always present), and Omnipotent (all powerful). Thank Him for sending His Son to die for your sins giving you the hope of an eternal life in Heaven when you die. Thank God for His creation. Thank Him for His daily strength and encouragement. God loves you so thank Him for it. The Psalms are filled with verses of thankfulness begin searching them today and when you are down reflect on passages that you have read in the past. Psalm 100:4 says *"Enter into his gates with thanksgiving, and into his courts with praise: be thankful unto him, and bless his name."* Be thankful today!

 # Going Further

In one or two sentences describe what Psalm 100:4 means to you?

How has Psalm 100:4 helped you on your single mom journey?

Make a list of 2-5 people that have been a blessing to your life in the past year then give them some form of thank you note through email, social networking, standard mail, text message, phone call, or whatever type of message you are comfortable with. The key is to always be thankful to anyone that helps you in any way.

In one sentence define thankfulness.

Write a thank you note to God for all He has done <u>for your children</u> during your single mom journey.

Write a thank you note to God for all He has done <u>for you</u> during your single mom journey.

Take Action

Make a list numbering 1-10 and then write 10 things that you have to be thankful for today. From this day forward when days are tough and you are not feeling thankful make another list. This discipline will quickly take you from self-pity to praising God for all of the amazing things He has done!

Prayer Time

Prayer Requests:

_____

_____

_____

_____

_____

_____

Suggested Prayer:

Dear Lord, I thank You for everything You have done for me from the blessings when I was a small child to the blessings in my life today; through You I am truly blessed...

The Single Mom Journey

The Single Mom Journey
Day 20

<u>Finding Security</u>

"My sheep hear my voice, and I know them, and they follow me: and I give unto them eternal life; and they shall never perish, neither shall any man pluck them out of my hand. My Father, which gave them me, is greater than all; and no man is able to pluck them out of my Father's hand." John 10:27-29

As single moms we could define our job as follows: "the act of stress, fear, worry, uncertainty, and anxiety, all resulting in a major lack of security!" You probably won't find this exact definition anywhere else, but in this book. As a single mom you may feel as though on most occasions your security account is drained. Most of the friends that I had on my single mom journey were married couples and when I would visit their homes I would get a feeling of security. I felt as though this security was not found in our home. No matter how hard I tried I felt as though I never could provide that security. One example of this lack of security was the front door and the windows of a house that we were renting. The door was an old wood door that had a large gap at the bottom and felt unsecure enough that a man could knock it down with a semi-powerful blow. The windows on this home could be easily unlocked from the outside. These two items and several other factors made for a feeling of insecurity in our home for a period of time. Most often women find their security in the man of the house and the barriers of her home and we had neither! I am here to testify though that God provided our security. God took care of us at this house and who better to put our security in? Looking back I believe the door could have been taken off of its hinges and the windows could have been left open and no one would have entered our home if it was not the will of God. I challenge you to not find your security in a man, in a home, or in any other earthly object, but find it in the comforting protection of God! So let us redefine being a single mom as follows: one who has the amazing privilege of learning to completely find their security in God alone.

-Connie

Challenge ~ Day 20

The following is one of the many definitions of security: *"something that secures or makes safe; protection; defense."*[12] Being a single mom you may often feel as if you are lacking security in your home. This is a normal feeling, but do not let a lack of security consume you, because whether you realize it or not, God is your security. God will take care of you at all times no matter what may happen to you. Three men of great faith (or great trust in God's security) in the Bible were Shadrach, Meshach, and Abednego (Daniel 3) who were kidnapped from their homes and taken as slaves into a foreign country. Despite all that had happened to them they still trusted God. One day they refused to bow down to a statue of Nebuchadnezzar, because they made the decision to follow the only true God. As a result for not bowing down and worshipping the statue, they were thrown into a fiery furnace. The furnace was so hot that it killed the soldiers that took Shadrach, Meshach, and Abednego to the furnace, but it was not hot enough to burn the men of God. If you read Daniel 3 it says that God was in the fire with them: *"I see four men loose, walking in the midst of the fire, and they have no hurt; and the form of the fourth is like the Son of God."*(vs.25) and God did not allow them to be harmed: *"upon whose bodies the fire had no power, nor was an hair of their head singed, neither were their coats changed, nor the smell of fire had passed on them."*(vs.27) Despite the fact that they were in the fiery furnace and no matter how hot it was God provided security for them. God did not let even one hair on their head be burned nor did they smell like the fire when they came out. This is a great example of how God provides protection to us today despite the fact that you may not feel as though you have "normal security"; trust in God to protect you and provide all of the security that you need.

 # Going Further

Read Daniel 3.

In one or two sentences describe what John 10:27-29 means to you?

How has John 10:27-29 helped you on your single mom journey?

In one sentence define security.

Connie had mentioned that the windows and the front door on her home gave her a lack of security? What in your life makes you feel unsafe or unsecure?

 # Take Action

Write a letter to God about your insecurities, and begin to trust Him to help you get through it.

📞 Prayer Time

Prayer Requests:

_____

_____

_____

_____

_____

_____

Suggested Prayer:

Dear Lord, I trust that You are my security. No matter how insecure I may feel, please help me to know that You are always with me and will always protect me...

The Single Mom Journey

The Single Mom Journey
Day 21

<u>Overcoming Abuse</u>

"He that dwelleth in the secret place of the most High shall abide under the shadow of the Almighty. I will say of the LORD, He is my refuge and my fortress: my God; in him will I trust." Psalm 91:1-2

One morning, while living in Las Vegas and pregnant with my oldest son, my husband and I had plans to visit with some friends for the day. While I was getting ready one of those friends called and as I was on the phone my husband, who had just come home drunk after a long night at the bar, began yelling at me and hitting me on my head and face. After several blows to the face my nose started bleeding and I ran outside to get away from him. He screamed for me to get back into the house. Then all of a sudden a stranger came up to our porch where I was standing and she put a blanket around me and took me to her car. This lady saw me from the road standing partially dressed and crying hysterically with blood pouring out of my nose. This stranger then took me to the local 7-11 and there we used the phone to call for help from family. I spent that night at my mother-in-law's home. To this day I wonder if the woman that rescued me was an angel unaware as mentioned in Hebrews 13:2. I experienced many years of physical and mental abuse and that were followed by many more years of scars and pain. So from one who has been abused if you are in that situation I urge you please seek help immediately before it is too late. Don't allow it to go on for years as I did. There are several forms of abuse you could be experiencing, but please remember God is there. God helped me overcome the years of abuse and scars that followed and He will do the same for you. I challenge you today to allow God to be your refuge and fortress.

–*Connie*

Challenge ~ Day 21

If you are reading this and are the victim of domestic violence, today is the day to make it stop! You have a choice. Do not let it go on any longer. Contact the authorities! Consider seeking out a trusted family member, a friend, or your local church to provide some help and encouragement. It is time for you to stand up for your safety and well-being. You must realize that you are a special person. You are special to God. God cares about you and what you are going through. You do not deserve to be subject to any type of abuse whether it be emotional or physical. It says in I Corinthians 15:10 *"But by the grace of God I am what I am: and his grace which was bestowed upon me was not in vain; but I laboured more abundantly than they all: yet not I, but the grace of God which was with me."* You are who God created you to be. Your entire makeup was designed by God and you are exceptional to Him! There are different types of abuse such as emotional and physical and it does not always come from a husband or a boyfriend. Stay away from people that bring you down spiritually and emotionally and anyone that tries to tear you down by making fun of you or making you feel like a loser. You are special and you deserve friends and family that treat you special. Surround yourself with encouraging people that will uplift you. It is a good practice to not spend time with people that bring you down or tear you down. There is a difference. People that bring you down are those that try to get you to participate in things that dishonor God. People that tear you down are those that make fun of you. Neither of these relationships are healthy. Start establishing healthy Christian relationships today!

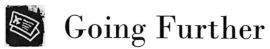 # Going Further

If you are the victim of domestic violence please make it stop today!

In one or two sentences describe what Psalm 91:1-2 means to you?

How has Psalm 91:1-2 helped you on your single mom journey?

In one or two sentences describe what I Corinthians 15:10 means to you?

How has I Corinthians 15:10 helped you on your single mom journey?

 # Take Action

Draw three columns and at the top of the columns label them in the following manner: good relationships, bad relationships, and future friends. Under the good column make a list of the good relationships in your life and begin working on making them better, pray for these people and that God would strengthen the relationship. Under the bad column make a list of the bad relationships (use initials or create a nickname that only you would recognize) in your life and begin working on how to either break them or to turn them into good, pray for these people that God would change their hearts. Under the future column make a list of the godly attributes that you want your future friends to have so you can avoid starting another bad relationship.

Prayer Time

Prayer Requests:

_____

_____

_____

_____

_____

_____

Suggested Prayer:

Dear Lord, thank You for the good relationships in my life and how You have used them to encourage and help me, please help me to break ties with or transform into good any bad relationships in my life, and please help me to avoid any other bad relationships in the future by knowing what attributes to look for...

The Single Mom Journey

The Single Mom Journey
Day 22

<u>Breaking The Cycle</u>

"I have no greater joy than to hear that my children walk in truth." III John 1:4

"Hurting people, hurt people." This statement is so true and sadly it is the reason so many single moms fall apart while raising their children and then their children repeat this process. As single moms we have been hurt, knocked down, bruised, and sometimes destroyed. Many of our personal goals, dreams, and desires have been postponed or ruined. Regardless of what has happened to us, we must be strong for our children. As a single mom we are raising fatherless children and if you are not aware, this issue is destroying the lives of young people every year. The following quote is one of many that are available that may allow you to see what we need to fight against: *"Fatherless Children are at a dramatically greater risk of drug and alcohol abuse, mental illness, suicide, poor educational performance, teen pregnancy, and criminality."*[13] You cannot let this statistic or any other statistics scare you along your single mom journey, we must persevere! We must fight for our child's life! I am speaking from experience when I say we must get past our own hurt and work hard to save our children from becoming a statistic. We must break the cycle! The Bible says *"I have no greater joy than to hear that my children walk in truth."* Make this your goal and passion to see your children walk in a close relationship with their Heavenly Father. They need you and you can help them! Get your children in Church, read the Bible and pray with them, fill your home with godly music and entertainment, and surround them with godly influences. Pray for your children on a daily basis asking God to not allow them to fall into the statistics of fatherlessness. I challenge you to overcome your hurt, put God first then your children, and be consumed with a passion to see them succeed in their Christian walk. If you do this, everything else should come together.

-Connie

Challenge ~ Day 22

What is your opinion on history? Do or did you enjoy it in school? Some individuals enjoy learning history and they see the value in learning it, but others are simply not that interested. Regardless of whether you enjoy it now or not, most likely the older you will get the more interesting you will find it to be. It is filled with real life stories of war, love, peace, happiness, tragedy, and much more. Parts of history are used as examples in sermons, speeches, and presentations to clarify a specific point or topic. Many of the most popular and powerful films in Hollywood are drawn from historical events. One of the most important aspects of history is that it is a resource for all individuals to use in order to learn from examples. You can find consequences, trials, and adversity that were developed from the actions of historians. This allows us to change our methods of how we may deal with events that may happen today. Even the President of the United States looks at historical situations before he may react to a current event, because the saying is true, "hind sight see's 20/20." Which means that when you know the outcome or what the results will be from a choice or decision that you are about to make, you will have a better idea of what kind of decision to choose. I Corinthians 3:13-17 shows us that we as individuals solely answer for ourselves in God's eyes. Despite what others do or have done in their own lives, it is our responsibility to manage our lives according to God's will! As a single mom you have a responsibility to strive to break the cycle for your children, enabling them to the best of your ability to not have a broken home in their future. III John 1:4 says: *"I have no greater joy than to hear that my children walk in truth."* Make this verse your goal today!

 # Going Further

In one or two sentences describe what III John 1:4 means to you?

How has III John 1:4 helped you on your single mom journey?

Date Night! That is right it is time for a date and with the most special people in your life, your children. Take some time right now to get all of the plans for the special date or dates lined up! To ensure the success of this event please try to fulfill the following instructions:

Date Night Details:

Venue: Set up a date with your child or children within the next week. Make plans to have a nice dinner at home or go to a nice restaurant, whichever you can afford. It doesn't have to be expensive, but the most important thing is to show your child that you really put some thought and effort into this. Within your budget work hard to make it special!

Objective: A time for you to talk to your children about a Biblical view of marriage.

Theme Verse: Ecclesiastes 4:9-10 *"Two are better than one; because they have a good reward for their labour. For if they fall, the one will lift up his fellow: but woe to him that is alone when he falleth; for he hath not another to help him up."*

Goal: To teach your children about what a Biblical Marriage is, and what they can have in the future.

What to Talk About: What are your thoughts on marriage? In today's society many individuals have a twisted view of marriage. There are several examples of what our society teaches us about marriage, but as a Christian you must have a Biblical view of it. In Genesis 2:18,21-24 we see the first marriage that ever took place. God created marriage and we as humans have no authority to change what the Lord established. The ideal situation would be for you to experience and watch how a healthy couple such as a mother and father get along and interact with one another, but you have to use what you have. God will bring couples into your children's lives that will be godly examples for them, and they can pick the pieces out of each of their relationships of how they think a marriage should be, but it is good for them to get some instruction from you as well. If they are young make sure you keep it at their level and you may want to abstain from talking to them about the birds and the bees just yet, but it is your call as their parent. Whatever their age is spend this date night teaching them something about a Biblical view of marriage for at least a few minutes. The rest of the date can be just a time to have fun with them! When your children begin dating, teach them to remember that they belong to God, and not their boyfriend, girlfriend, or even their fiancé. No one should act as if they have ownership of them, and if this happens, they should end the relationship right away. Sex is something God created for married couples and married couples only.   Whomever God brings into their life, the following are a few guidelines they should follow:

1. **Put God first** – God should always be the first priority in their life.
2. **Respect them** – Their boyfriend or girlfriend is not their possession, he or she belongs to God, and the same goes with how they should view your children.
3. **Pray** – Pray daily for the spouse that God will have you marry.
4. **Read the Bible** – Seek God's will through His Scriptures.
5. **Don't rush anything** – *"Your body is the temple of the Holy Ghost."* (I Corinthians 6:19)

Take Action

Make a list of the habits, behaviors, or past failures of your own or of your family members that you do not want your children to obtain then make a plan to help your children break the cycle.

Prayer Time

Prayer Requests:

_____

_____

_____

_____

_____

_____

Suggested Prayer:

Dear Lord, I pray that You will help me to model my life after Your will today. I thank You for giving me the opportunity and time to learn from examples of good and bad. Please help me to find some good examples in my life from history or in the Bible that I may model my life after...

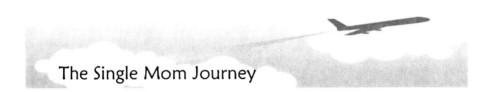

The Single Mom Journey

The Single Mom Journey
Day 23

God Brings Happiness

"Thou wilt shew me the path of life: in thy presence is fulness of joy; at thy right hand there are pleasures for evermore." Psalm 16:11

The day that I got married I was very happy and I thought this happiness would continue for the rest of my life. There were happy moments in our marriage and there were unhappy moments. Then the day came when I received divorce papers from my husband, and needless to say, I became very unhappy. After receiving these papers I called the leader of my church's women's Bible study to ask her to pray for me and she said something similar to the following: "you have to remember that happiness can only come from God not from people, because people will disappoint you and God won't." This statement is so very true and I have seen it time and time again how people and things of this earth in general will disappoint you and often bring sadness and despair. But the Bible tells us in Hebrews 13:8 *"Jesus Christ the same yesterday, and today, and for ever."* He was there for you before, He is here for you now, and He will be there for you in the future. He will never disappoint you! No earthly offering can bring the level of joy that God can provide to your life if you just let Him. I challenge you today to find your happiness in God because with Him it will last for eternity!

–Connie

Challenge ~ Day 23

What is your definition of true happiness? Something probably came to your mind. Was it money? Was it a new car? Was it a big house? Was it a vacation? Regardless of what it was did it have anything to do with God? In the heart touching movie *The Pursuit of Happiness* Will Smith plays a loving father that would do anything to provide for his family. It shows him striving to make ends meet as a salesman and in addition striving to further himself by fulfilling an internship that might eventually provide him with a very lucrative job. He truly went to drastic measures to make this happen! This movie was based on a real life story of a man that truly pursued happiness through financial gain. Financial gain is not wrong, but when that is your only pursuit in life there is still emptiness present. True and lasting happiness is only found from God. In Psalm 16:11 it says *"Thou wilt shew me the path of life: in thy presence is fulness of joy; at thy right hand there are pleasures for evermore."* Happiness from God lasts forever! Monetary, relational, mental, emotional, and other types of happiness are good and you should pursue them, but make sure that the pursuit of happiness from God is in the center of all of it! An individual that pursues only earthly happiness could be compared to someone taking a trip to Walt Disney World. For most people just reading the words Walt Disney World it brings thoughts of peace, excitement, happiness, and other such comforting terms. Walt Disney World is a place of fun, relaxation, families, and much more. Most everyone has a desire to go there and when they actually get to visit they are amazed at all of its wonders. The mysterious imaginative nature of this place brings about childhood feelings, and it is a truly wonderful experience, but everyone's trip to this place eventually comes to an end and you have to go home. You see one can pursue only the pleasures of this world for their entire life, but eventually it will come to an end. What then? If you pursue happiness from God in all you do this is a happiness that will last for eternity!

 # Going Further

In one or two sentences describe what Psalm 16:11 means to you?

How has Psalm 16:11 helped you on your single mom journey?

In one sentence define happiness.

Write a paragraph about someone (friend, family member, celebrity, Bible character, etc.) who pursued only earthly happiness and it kept them from reaching their full potential. Why did their pursuit not include God? What could they have done differently? What was the end result?

Write a paragraph about someone (friend, family member, celebrity, Bible character, etc.) whose pursuits of happiness were centered on God. Why and how did they put God at the center of their pursuits? What was the end result? How can you learn from their example?

Take Action

What does your pursuit of happiness include? Write a paragraph on what you are pursuing for your future and regardless of what it is make sure God is the center of it. Please understand that the pursuit of financial gain is not wrong, but make sure that God is in all that you are trying to do!

Prayer Time

Prayer Requests:

_____

_____

_____

_____

_____

_____

Suggested Prayer:

Dear Lord, please help me to seek happiness from You in everything that I do…

The Single Mom Journey

THE TRIP - WEEK 3

Days 24-30

The Single Mom Journey
Day 24

<u>Confidence</u>

"Being confident of this very thing, that he which hath begun a good work in you will perform it until the day of Jesus Christ." Philippians 1:6

Since you are reading this book I am assuming that you are a single mom that is trying to figure out this whole journey and how to make sure you and your children come out on top. On my single mom journey I had a continual lack of confidence. When I would think of going at it alone it made me fearful and brought about feelings of inferiority. The thought of doing everything for my children all alone scared me. Regardless of my lack of confidence, God was always there for me and even when I did not realize it, brought the confidence that I needed. The Bible says that *"he which hath begun a good work in you will perform it until the day of Jesus Christ."* This is very true; God will do it if you just let Him. Joseph, the great grandson of Abraham, was given a tough journey as well. It tells us in Genesis 37 that when Joseph was a young man his brothers hated him so much that they plotted to kill him but instead sold him into slavery. This was just the beginning of the tough road that Joseph had to travel before being triumphant. Throughout all of Joseph's trials and tribulations he persevered, because his confidence was in the Lord and it tells us in a few verses in Genesis 39 that *"the Lord was with Joseph."* This is true for you and your journey. The Lord is with you if you will continue to seek Him and live for Him. I challenge you today to find your confidence in God, because only through Him will you be able to do it!

–Connie

Challenge ~ Day 24

Abraham Lincoln was a great man. Not only was he a great president, but he also is given credit for the abolition of slavery in the United States. Despite his great accomplishments and prestigious positions, honest Abe was not always a success. In fact, he had run for the United States Senate on two occasions and did not win. At this time in his life, he was probably feeling defeated and he probably had a lack of confidence. Despite all of the great things he accomplished later in life, these losses were probably very discouraging. Despite his failures he remained confident, though it was probably not easy, and eventually became the President of the United States.[14] Sometimes you may feel overwhelmed and not have any confidence at all, but there is hope. Luke 1:37 shows us that *"For with God nothing shall be impossible."* God created this earth. He created it and is the Master of everything. He is our Guide, our Deliverer, and our Strength. He sent His Son to die for our sins on the cross to save us from an eternity in Hell. He is Almighty, All Powerful. Be confident in the Lord for His grace is sufficient. Trust God today and let Him alone be your confidence.

 # Going Further

In one or two sentences describe what Philippians 1:6 means to you?

How has Philippians 1:6 helped you on your single mom journey?

In one sentence define confidence.

Have you claimed a Bible verse on confidence? A verse that you could quote when things seem impossible? Take some time to search the Scriptures if you do not already have one.

Read through Genesis 37-50 and then write out 5-10 habits or characteristics of Joseph that you could practice in your own life.

Take Action

Make a list of the top 10 things in your life that seem to be impossible. Begin praying for these things daily until they are no longer impossible.

Prayer Time

Prayer Requests:

_____

_____

_____

_____

_____

_____

Suggested Prayer:

Dear Lord, I put my trust in You. Please help me to be confident in You in the good and the bad times. I trust You with my life and only through You am I able to move forward each day...

The Single Mom Journey

The Single Mom Journey
Day 25

Father's Day

"From the end of the earth will I cry unto thee, when my heart is overwhelmed: lead me to the rock that is higher than I." Psalm 61:2

When I was growing up I had a close relationship with my father and this close relationship continued on throughout my adult years. When I was raising my children it broke my heart that they did not have the opportunity to have this type of relationship. These thoughts came especially relevant on Father's Day. This day is hard for every boy and girl that is growing up without a father in their life. In Church on Father's Day preachers typically preach on the image of a good father and the Sunday school teachers have a lesson and sometimes a craft to celebrate the child's father. This was often painful for my children. Then came the time when my father passed away and now Father's Day was hard for me too. I do not recommend this, but I remember there were times after my father passed away that we would skip church on Father's Day, because the pain was too great to bear. I would try to do what I could to make the day special for my children to help get their minds off of their lack of a father, because I knew it was painful. We did not have much money, but I would try to take their minds off this painful day by doing small things such as surrounding them by family or by going and getting ice cream or something similar. Father's Day will most likely be hard for your family every year so plan some items for the day that might help ease the pain, and don't forget that when your heart is overwhelmed trust in God to be your strength, because He truly is a Father to the fatherless!

-Connie

Challenge ~ Day 25

Everyone loves Holidays! Most are filled with joy, happiness, and they sometimes even include a few days off of school or work. They are a time to share and reflect on the meaning of that special day. Christmas is a day to remember the Birth of Jesus Christ and Easter is when we remember His death, burial, and resurrection. Valentine's Day we take some extra time to express how we feel about the ones we love. On the Fourth of July we remember our independence in the United States of America and that we are free to live, and most importantly, that we have religious freedom. New Year's gives us a fresh slate to complete our goals. There are many holidays throughout the year, but one that plagues fatherless families is Father's Day. For many fatherless families this day brings sadness and despair. For some it might be viewed as too overwhelming to bear. Whatever this day brings to you or you and your children, you can and will get through it. In Psalm 61:2, David wrote *"From the end of the earth will I cry unto thee, when my heart is overwhelmed: lead me to the rock that is higher than I."* Even David had days when he too was overwhelmed, but he trusted God to get him through those tough times. If you and your children are overwhelmed on Father's Day seek the Lord for strength and comfort. According to Romans 8:15: *"For ye have not received the spirit of bondage again to fear; but ye have received the Spirit of adoption, whereby we cry, Abba, Father."* we do have something to celebrate on Father's Day, our Abba Father!

 # Going Further

In one or two sentences describe what Psalm 61:2 means to you?

How has Psalm 61:2 helped you on your single mom journey?

How will you teach your children that God is their Abba Father? How will you remind them of this verse, especially on hard days such as Father's Day? Consider helping your children memorize this verse.

What are some ways that you could make Father's Day fun for your children? Try to plan some yearly traditions for this day to help your children take their mind off of it. Make it a day where you celebrate that God is your Father. Celebrate that. Make that your focus.

 # Take Action

Make a list of the reasons that Father's Day is hard for you and your children. Pray daily that God will give you strength and comfort to get through the upcoming Father's Day and any other days that may overwhelm your family.

Prayer Time

Prayer Requests:

_____

_____

_____

_____

_____

_____

Suggested Prayer:

Dear Lord I ask that You would please provide strength and comfort to my family on Father's Day and other days that we feel overwhelmed. I realize that only through You can we get through these things, and I ask that You will lead us to the rock that is higher than us...

The Single Mom Journey

The Single Mom Journey
Day 26

Mentors – For You

"If any of you lack wisdom, let him ask of God, that giveth to all men liberally, and upbraideth not; and it shall be given him." James 1:5

I must say that I have been blessed through the past several years with several loyal friends and family members. They were there for me in times of need during my single mom journey. As I look back now I must say that each one of these friends and family members helped me in different ways throughout this journey. When I became a single mom there weren't a lot of people that understood what I was going through. I did have one friend that was on a single mom journey too; our families often did things together, and she was a great friend too. Nevertheless, I still had to find some mentors/wise counsel that I could seek guidance and direction from. I found some of the best mentors through my church. These women, the majority of which were pastor's wives, gave me guidance and direction in a Biblical perspective for my single mom journey. These women always let me know that they were available if I ever needed to talk about anything. Knowing I had these valuable resources to help me was a tremendous comfort. There were times that I was so overwhelmed and I honestly felt as if I was not going to make it on my single mom journey. I knew that if I did not seek some wise counsel that I would derail on my journey letting my family and myself down. These were the times when those women would counsel me on the hard topics of finances, parenting, loneliness, bitterness, and many other aspects of how to live a successful Christian life. If it was not for those women I may have derailed on my journey. I challenge you to find some godly women that you can go to for advice and encouragement along your single mom journey. You do not have to do it all alone. And speaking from experience mentors are life savers!

-Connie

Challenge ~ Day 26

Even though you are a single mom in every situation there is always a positive element that needs to be addressed: mentors. One of the most encouraging things a person can have in their life is a mentor. What truly is a mentor? A definition of a good mentor would be the following: A godly influence that one is able to watch, imitate, and gain knowledge from in a positive manner. Whether direct or indirect a mentor helps guide the individual in the right path of life. Let me tell you about a boy named George. When George was eleven years old his father died. Soon after his father died his older brother became the hero and mentor for George. George is a man that every American has heard of. He accomplished great things in his lifetime. This boy later became known as the Father of the United States of America: George Washington. Everyone has seen this great man's face on either the quarter or a one dollar bill. Despite the fatherless journey in George Washington's life he still had great success. One of the keys to George Washington's success was that he had a mentor in his life. After his father died his older half-brother became a hero and mentor to him.[15] Just like George Washington, you too need to seek for a mentor in your life. A godly mentor will help you make the right decisions, provide encouragement, and make your single mom journey not feel so alone. Begin praying today, asking God that He may provide a mentor for you, and if you already have a mentor thank God for them! *"If any of you lack wisdom, let him ask of God, that giveth to all men liberally, and upbraideth not; and it shall be given him."* James 1:5

 # Going Further

In one or two sentences describe what James 1:5 means to you?

How has James 1:5 helped you on your single mom journey?

In one sentence define mentor.

Make a list of 5-10 godly Christian women in your life that could mentor you.

Make a list of anything that would keep you from pursuing a mentor. If you already have a mentor, take some time to write a thank you letter to her.

 # Take Action

Make a list of the characteristics that you would look for in a mentor for yourself. For example, you may want a person that will teach you about life, how to handle finances, etc. Begin praying and asking God to provide a mentor that matches these characteristics and one that you can model your life after.

Prayer Time

Prayer Requests:

_____
_____
_____
_____
_____
_____

Suggested Prayer:

Dear Lord, I ask that You will bring into my life a Christian that will teach me life lessons that I have not yet learned or may need help developing, and who will challenge me to live a life that is honoring and pleasing to You...

The Single Mom Journey

The Single Mom Journey
Day 27

Mentors – For Your Children

"Pure religion and undefiled before God and the Father is this, To visit the fatherless and widows in their affliction, and to keep himself unspotted from the world." James 1:27

Several statistics show that children from at-risk homes have a greater chance of turning out on a successful life path if they have a positive mentor in their life. As a Christian, I believe that Christian mentors can make an eternal impact on a young person's life. This is not to say that I did not have the ability to make an impact on my children's lives, but they also needed some other individuals, especially manly examples that could help shape them with Biblical life values. When I think about mentoring and the affects that it had on my own children I have mixed emotions, because my oldest son lacked mentors, but my daughter and especially my younger son were blessed with an abundance of mentors. When my oldest son was growing up I tried hard to find him a good Christian mentor, but he only had a few individuals take interest in him on a few occasions. This was sad but true. When it came to my younger two it was a completely different scenario, and I remember constantly driving them from one godly family's house to the next. They were surrounded by individuals that cared about them and showed them that they were truly loved. These mentors helped teach my children character, integrity, forgiveness, confidence, purity, and how to live a successful Christian life. They showed my children how to have a Biblical marriage, how to handle finances wisely, how to work ethically, how to find godly friendships, how to overcome the temptation of this world, and much more. Now do not get me wrong, my children were not perfect nor were their mentors, but without these relationships I am afraid to think about who my children would be today. I am truly thankful that God allowed these relationships to grow! I challenge you to strive to find godly mentors to help guide your children on their fatherless journey, because they cannot afford for you not to.

-Connie

Challenge ~ Day 27

Your children will have the opportunity to have both direct and indirect mentors. They can switch in and out at different points in their life. They may be closer to one or another. Direct mentors are those men and women that do things for them exactly at this moment. They are purposefully trying to make a difference in their life as well. Indirect mentors are those men and women that your children watch and begin to follow certain life patterns that they may possess in their lives. This could be an employer, a pastor, a teacher, a coach, a relative, or someone else. The exciting thing about your situation is that your children have the ability to pick up the best qualities of the mentors in their life. They have the chance to learn completely different things from each of them. Items such as: how to work, how to respect authority, how to handle money, how to treat girls (boys), how to be treated by boys (girls), and the list goes on. Some of the things they will learn will be a mixture of what a couple of their mentors will teach them. Having mentors can be fun if they make it that way. A key part in having mentors is accepting that they truly are fatherless, understanding that they cannot learn some things on their own, and realizing that as a single mother there are some things that you may not be able to teach them. Do not fret, because there are men and women of God in your local community that will heed to the teaching of James 1:27 where it says *"To visit the fatherless"*; just continue to trust that God will provide a mentor until their mentors come along.

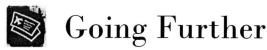 # Going Further

In one or two sentences describe what James 1:27 means to you?

How has James 1:27 helped you on your single mom journey?

Life Factors Ministries believes that mentoring saves lives! Through Christian mentoring children and teens are able to receive some additional guidance to help them on their broken home journey. To find out details on how to get a mentoring program started at your church please visit lifefactors.org!

Make a list of the men and women that you would consider to be mentors or even potential mentors for your children. If you include a current mentor in your list write out the things that you think they could learn from that mentor. Make a list of things that this mentor has already taught them.

Name	Characteristics of a godly mentor/How they have already helped?

If you included a possible mentor write out ways that your children could try to become closer to them. An example of this would be to ask the potential mentor to teach your son how to change oil in a car or if she wants to get together for coffee with your daughter and talk. Everything is worth a try. If your children get turned down by a mentor, don't worry about it. Just pray and ask God that He will give them the mentors that they are supposed to have. Sit back and watch how God works. He may give them a mentor, or He may even bring them closer to a family member or a current friend.

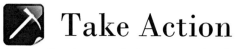 # Take Action

Write a thank you note to anyone that has mentored your children in any capacity then give it to them through a letter, email, phone call, etc. Always make sure you take the time to thank those who have helped and encouraged you and your family.

✆ Prayer Time

Prayer Requests:

_____

_____

_____

_____

_____

_____

Suggested Prayer:

Dear Lord, I pray trusting that You will work on a Christian mentor's heart to have the desire to teach my children the things that they need to learn to become men and women of You...

The Single Mom Journey

The Single Mom Journey
Day 28

Church

"Not forsaking the assembling of ourselves together, as the manner of some is: but exhorting one another: and so much the more, as ye see the day approaching." Hebrews 10:25

When I think of the word "church" I think of a place of refuge, because throughout the majority of my single mom journey it has been a comforting place. As I mentioned on day one when I was growing up my father made us go to church almost every Sunday. Back then church was a fun place where my sister and I were members of the choir, I played specials on the organ, and it always made me feel good to attend. After receiving Jesus Christ as my personal Savior church became so much more to me. Before my husband left I was invited by some of my cousins to attend the church that I am still a member of. To sum up my past 25 plus years at this church would be - no regrets. I have no regrets for getting myself and my children plugged into this safe and healthy environment. Now sure there were times when I did not understand the actions of some of this church's members and staff, but this did not steer me from my purpose of being there and that was to grow myself and my family in the knowledge of God's Word. As a single mom we need a place to go where we can get fueled up for the trials of our journey. We need this weekly or semiweekly fueling and so do our children. Also, in most churches there are separate programs for the children and adults. Moms this is a chance for you to put your child or teenager into a safe environment and for you to get some time alone to grow in the Lord. I challenge you, if you are not already, to get your family plugged into a Bible preaching and salvation teaching church today, because you cannot function properly without the fuel that you will receive.

-Connie

Challenge ~ Day 28

When you hear the word "church" what comes to your mind? You may think of Easter and Christmas because that is honestly the only time you attend. You may be thinking of your weekly routine because this word is in your schedule on a consistent basis. You may be thinking of the good or bad memories that you have had in a church during your childhood, teen, or adult years. Regardless of your thoughts, church is a very important part to growing as a Christian and to conquer your single mom journey. You need church, that is right, you need it. You cannot afford to not go to church. As a single mother you need this time of refueling on a weekly or semiweekly basis. Also, God commands us in Hebrews 10:25 to *"not forsaking the assembling of ourselves together,"* which means if you are able to go to church, then go to church. The next part of this verse says *"but exhorting one another: and so much the more, as ye see the day approaching"*, at church you will be challenged and find hope through the preaching and teaching of God's word to live a consistent walk for God and you will find encouragement and help for your single mom journey. In addition, your children will be given Biblical instruction that is a priceless resource on their fatherless journey. When picking a church look for one that holds sound doctrine, this means find a church that believes and teaches according to what the Bible says. There are a lot of good churches out there but sadly there are also some that do not follow the Biblical model of a Church and there are those that do not preach and teach according to the Word of God. If you are unsure as to which church to attend you can contact Life Factors Ministries at info@lifefactors.org and we will give you some recommendations on some Bible believing churches in your neighborhood. When you do find your church do not just attend, but rather pour yourself and your children into it every opportunity that they offer!

 # Going Further

In one or two sentences describe what Hebrews 10:25 means to you?

How has Hebrews 10:25 helped you on your single mom journey?

In one sentence define church.

If you do not attend a church faithfully make a list of anything that is keeping you from attending church then pray and ask God to help you to overcome these things and to guide you to the church that He wants you to attend.

 # Take Action

If you do not currently have a church begin looking for one, make a list of friends and family members that attend church and consider visiting with them. If you need help in finding a church please do not hesitate to contact Life Factors Ministries today at info@lifefactors.org! If you do have a church, list ways you and your family could be more involved. If you are already heavily involved in your local church then we commend you! Write a thank you note to God for the church He has brought into your life!

Prayer Time

Prayer Requests:

_____

_____

_____

_____

_____

_____

Suggested Prayer:

Dear Lord, help me to follow Your Scriptures where it says "not forsaking the assembling of ourselves together," help me to keep my family involved in a local church...

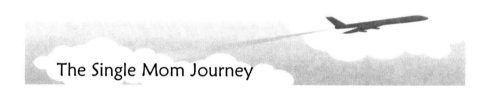

The Single Mom Journey

The Single Mom Journey
Day 29

Setting Goals

"Delight thyself also in the LORD; and he shall give thee the desires of thine heart. Commit thy way unto the LORD; trust also in him; and he shall bring it to pass." Psalm 37:4-5

Many years ago I was doing some volunteer work at the private Christian school my children were attending and the principal's wife asked me to go to lunch with her. While at the diner we were talking and she looked at me and said, "My husband and I feel that you are doing a great job raising your kids." This was something I needed to hear that day, and I was very surprised that she said it. Her words meant so much to me because at that time in my life my main goal was to do a great job raising my children. I had a burden that they would turn out in a God-honoring manner. Let me ask you, what is or are your goals for your children? Do you have a passion and a desire to see them succeed? Since you are reading this book I am sure that it is your goal and most likely your strongest desire to succeed on your single mom journey, and by setting goals it will be much easier to make sure it happens. Set goals for yourself and your children regarding the following: Christian walk, grades, college aspirations, relationships, future accomplishments, and whatever else God leads you to. Before setting these goals pray asking God to give you the goals that He wants you to have for your children and for your own life, and then when you have your list of goals pray over them often. I challenge you today to set some goals no matter how few or how many you may come up with, then give them to God, and trust Him to bring them to fruition in the manner that He deems best.

–Connie

Challenge ~ Day 29

Everyone has goals in life: some have good goals, some have bad goals, some have a lot of goals, some have few goals, some have set high goals, and some have set mediocre goals. What kind of goals have you set for yourself so far in your life? Setting goals is very important to a successful life journey. You do not have to know where you will be at in 10 years, what next year will bring, or even what will take place next month, but you should still set goals for the immediate and long-term future. For example, planning or purposing in your heart that you will do your best at work before it starts each day is a way of setting an immediate goal. Deciding that you will be a pure example in front of your children each day and purposing that this will not change is an example of both an immediate and a long-term goal. Praying and asking God to open your heart and teach you something before church is an example of setting an immediate goal. Setting goals is deciding in the present how you want your life to be in the future. Sometimes your goals may not turn out exactly how you imagined, but Psalm 37:4-5 tells us that as long as you are delighting in the Lord and committing your life to Him, He will guide you to the life He wants you to have. As a single mom you should set goals for your children regarding: their relationship with God, college aspirations, future spouse, future occupation, and whatever else God lays on your heart. Pray and ask God today to help you establish goals for yourself and for your children that are honoring to Him.

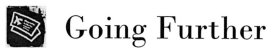 # Going Further

In one or two sentences describe what Psalm 37:4-5 means to you?

How has Psalm 37:4-5 helped you on your single mom journey?

In one sentence define goals.

Is there anything that keeps you from setting goals?

Make a list of 10 goals for the next month, 10 goals for the next year, and 10 goals for the next five years <u>for yourself</u>. Make goals on having a pure family, succeeding at your job or in school, growing as a Christian, and whatever else the Lord leads you to.

Next Month – 10 Goals:

Next Year – 10 Goals:

Next Five Years – 10 Goals:

Make a list of 10 goals for the next month, 10 goals for the next year, and 10 goals for the next five years <u>for your children</u>. Make goals for their Christian walk, grades, college aspirations, relationships, future accomplishments, and whatever else God leads you to.

Next Month – 10 Goals:

Next Year – 10 Goals:

Next Five Years – 10 Goals:

Take Action

Write a letter to God asking Him to help you accomplish the goals which you have set for yourself and for your children.

Prayer Time

Prayer Requests:

_____

_____

_____

_____

_____

_____

Suggested Prayer:

Dear Lord, please help me today to establish goals for my family that are honoring and pleasing to You. Help me to please You with the life and family which You have given to me...

The Single Mom Journey

The Single Mom Journey
Day 30

Success

"Whether therefore ye eat, or drink, or whatsoever ye do, do all to the glory of God."
I Corinthians 10:31

Congratulations! You made it! Today is the last day on the path to conquering your single mom journey, well okay maybe not, but I wanted to be the first to congratulate you on finishing this single mom life guide! You have done a great job, and I am very proud of you! I am so excited that you made it. I am sure you will agree that working through these issues was not the easiest thing that you have done, but they needed to be accomplished. In the future you may even have to remind yourself of God's love and strength to get you through a difficulty in life. One of my favorite hymns is "When We See Christ" and the following are some of the amazing lyrics:

"It will be worth it all when we see Jesus,
Life's trials will seem so small when we see Christ;
One glimpse of His dear face all sorrow will erase,
So bravely run the race till we see Christ."[16]

It will all be worth it in the end! I am speaking from experience on this and I promise you will not regret successfully completing this single mom journey that you are on. Even to this day I get compliments on how my now grownup children turned out, and I can honestly say looking back that it is only by the Grace of God that I made it on my single mom journey. A great life application verse is I Thessalonians 5:24 *"Faithful is he that calleth you, who also will do it."* Success is completing what you have committed to: whether it be a job, relationship, chore, or whatever it may be if you commit to something strive to complete it. I challenge you today to continue on a successful path along your single mom journey, because I assure you that you will not regret it!
-*Connie*

Challenge ~ Day 30

Noah's Ark and the story of the Flood have become known throughout the world. For many it is an intriguing story that people consider to be fiction. However, Noah was a real man, and the flood that covered the earth actually did happen. Speculators might have their reasons for not believing: maybe they cannot comprehend someone giving several years of their life to God to build an Ark, or maybe they cannot comprehend the fact that every man besides Noah's family was wiped off the face of the earth. It could be that they do not understand how one could save at least two of every kind of animal or that a boat could be built back then that would make it through such a storm. There are many things concerning Noah's journey, the construction of the ark, and the actual flood that we may have a hard time understanding. Noah probably struggled with understanding it as well, but in the end, it was a success. Noah was not perfect, but he did what God had told him to do. He took the burden of a large problem upon his shoulders, and this is what Hebrews 11:7 says about him: *"By faith Noah, being warned of God of things not seen as yet, moved with fear, prepared an ark to the saving of his house; by the which he condemned the world, and became heir of the righteousness which is by faith."* What about you? Right now your flood is your single mom journey, and you must not give up as you build the big boat to survive. You have to continue on with the project until it is completed. At Life Factors Ministries we are praying that you will grow strong in the Lord as you continue on in your single mom journey.

 # Going Further

In one or two sentences describe what I Corinthians 10:31 means to you?

How has I Corinthians 10:31 helped you on your single mom journey?

In one sentence define success.

Noah may have struggled with understanding part of his journey in building the Ark, but he kept at it. What are 2-3 things that you struggle with understanding on your single mom journey?

174

Write a paragraph about someone (friend, family member, celebrity, Bible character, etc.) who was not able to fulfill the calling on their life. Why did they fail? What could they have done differently? What was the end result?

Write a paragraph about someone (friend, family member, celebrity, Bible character, etc.) who was successful on their life path. What was the reason for their success? What was the end result? How can you learn from their example?

Take Action

Write out the things that you will need to continue to work through on your single mom journey to be certain that you will have true success. Pray, asking God to give you wisdom and guidance along your journey.

📞 Prayer Time

Prayer Requests:

_____
_____
_____
_____
_____
_____

Suggested Prayer:

Dear Lord, I thank You for giving me the ability to finish this devotional and life guide. I thank You for the lessons that You have taught me and I ask that You would please help me to live a successful life according to Your will...

The Single Mom Journey

lifefactors.org

LIFE FACTORS MINISTRIES
preventing & helping broken homes

Visit our website to find additional helpful resources! We are here for you and want to help you along your single mom journey! Check out the site today!

ADDITIONAL RESOURCES

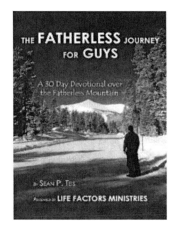

THE FATHERLESS JOURNEY for GUYS

The Fatherless Journey Devotional Book is a must have for every fatherless young man. It is a journey over your individual fatherless mountain. This life guide will help strengthen you to continue on with life despite your circumstances. Being fatherless, you are faced with life obstacles that many fathered individuals do not understand. In addition to the obstacles, there are several statistics stacked against you, and this devotional is designed to guide you away from being another one of the statistics. Each day of this journey is filled with practical, yet Scriptural guidance, that will enable you to live a life of success. Available at *lifefactors.org*.

THE FATHERLESS JOURNEY for GIRLS

The Fatherless Journey Devotional Book is a must have for every fatherless young lady. It is a guide for your individual fatherless journey. This life guide will help strengthen you to continue on with life despite your circumstances. Being fatherless, you are faced with life obstacles that many fathered individuals do not understand. In addition to the obstacles, there are several statistics stacked against you, and this devotional is designed to guide you away from becoming another one of the statistics. Each day of this journey is filled with practical, yet Biblical guidance that will enable you to live a life of success. Sean P. Teis and April M. Yeager are siblings that grew up in a unique fatherless home, and they both realize that God brought them through it all. Available at *lifefactors.org*.

ADDITIONAL RESOURCES

DANIEL and DANA THE FATHERLESS DINOS

This Children's series introduces encouragement and hope for every fatherless young boy and girl making it a must read for any type of fatherless circumstance! These books provide Biblical instruction for what can be a hopeless situation. Daniel and Dana, though fictional characters, share real life experiences from a fatherless home that will relate to any fatherless child. Daniel and Dana The Fatherless Dino's series is a useful tool for parents, grandparents, extended family, teachers, pastors, mentors, and anyone else that desires to help and encourage a fatherless child. Available at *lifefactors.org*.

MENTORING

Life Factors Ministries believes that mentoring saves lives! Through Christian

 mentoring children and teens are able to receive some additional guidance to help them on their fatherless journey. If you or your children need a mentor or if you are interested in becoming a mentor please visit *lifefactors.org* to find additional information on how to get started today!

NOTES

Day 3:

1. http://www.webmd.com/depression/guide/depression-women
2. http://www.mayoclinic.com/health/depression/DS00175

Day 4:

3. "Gilligans Island Theme Song," http://www.lyricsmode.com/lyrics/g/gilligans_island/gilligans_island_theme_song.html.

Day 5:

4. http://www.hymnlyrics.org/newlyrics_a/andcanitbethatishouldgain.php

Day 7:

5. "Todd Beamer," http://en.wikipedia.org/wiki/Todd_Beamer.

Day 9:

6. Journal of the American Academy of Child and Adolescent Psychiatry 33 (1994)

Day 14:

7. Adrian Rogers

Day 15:

8. http://en.wikipedia.org/wiki/Andre_Agassi

Day 16:

9. Unknown

Day 17:

10. "Abort," http://thesaurus.com/browse/abort. 1 September 2012.

Day 19:

11. http://www.history.com/topics/thanksgiving

Day 20:

12. "Security," http://dictionary.reference.com/browse/security. 17 February 2011.

Day 22:

13. U.S. Department of Health and Human Services, National Center for Health Statistics, Survey on Child Health, Washington, DC, 1993.

Day 24:

14. "Abraham Lincoln," http://en.wikipedia.org/wiki/Abraham_Lincoln.

Day 26:

15. Joseph J. Ellis, *His Excellency: George Washington* (New York: Vintage Books, 2004). 7-10.

Day 30:

16. "When We See Christ,"http://www.hymnpod.com/2009/06/15/when-we-see-christ/

CPSIA information can be obtained
at www.ICGtesting.com
Printed in the USA
FFOW04n1632221217
44211434-43660FF